The Cook's Tale

Born in Norfolk in 1907, Nancy Jackman left school at fourteen and began work as a kitchen maid and then cook in a series of houses. Nancy died in 1989.

Tom Quinn is the editor of the *Country Landowner* magazine. He has written several books for small independent publishers. He has spent the past twenty years interviewing people who worked in domestic service, recording their life stories.

The Cook's Tale

Nancy Jackman with Tom Quinn

CORONET

First published in Great Britain in 2012 by Coronet
An imprint of Hodder & Stoughton
An Hachette UK company

First published in paperback in 2012

1

A CIP catalogue record for this title is available from the British Library

ISBN 978 1 444 73589 5
Ebook ISBN 9781444735901

Typeset in Sabon MT by Hewer Text UK Ltd, Edinburgh
Printed and bound by CPI Group (UK) Ltd, Croydon, CR0 4YY

Hodder & Stoughton policy is to use papers that are natural, renewable
and recyclable products and made from wood grown in sustainable forests.
The logging and manufacturing processes are expected to conform to the
environmental regulations of the country of origin.

Hodder & Stoughton Ltd
338 Euston Road
London NW1 3BH

www.hodder.co.uk

Introduction

A century ago the vast majority of poor country children grew up knowing their choices in life would be limited. In most cases they would have to work either in agriculture or, if they were girls, in domestic service. In the houses of the gentry, thirty or forty servants might be employed. In the biggest houses of all, two or three hundred servants might be needed to ensure a life of unimaginable luxury for a tiny number of wealthy individuals and their families.

The servants who cleaned the rooms and washed, ironed and mended the linen were important, but their work went largely unnoticed. The kitchen was very different. When you have a great deal of leisure time, eating becomes almost absurdly important. And country families with a position to keep up were judged on the quality of the food prepared for dinner parties and guests.

So for the leisured classes a good cook was among the most highly prized and best paid of all the servants, but to be a cook it was necessary to endure a gruelling apprenticeship as a kitchen maid. And if being a cook brought some status it did not bring wealth or freedom, as Nancy Jackman explains in this account of her extraordinary life.

I first met Nancy in 1985 in her beautifully kept two-up-two-down house in King's Lynn. A lifetime of hard physical work had given her a solidity and strength that she retained into old age. But she was also tremendously sunny and warm and she had something of the earth mother about her despite having no children herself. She delighted in the idea that every visitor was desperately in need of an enormous meal and endless cups of intensely sweet tea.

She told me that, looking back, she realised how lucky she had been in two respects: she had been loved by her parents and she had known the countryside before the coming of the motor car. She was particularly close to her father whose stories lit up her childhood and I realised that she had inherited his storytelling gift to a remarkable degree. Her account of the distant past, whether describing her happy childhood wandering the fields and hedgerows or her terrible experience as a skivvy, had all the clarity of cinema.

Over the next few years, until her death in 1989, I visited Nancy on a number of occasions. She loved the fact that someone was interested in her life and that all that she had experienced would not be lost when she was no longer around. But she hated the idea that people would think she was bitter about her life. One of the last things she said to me was: 'I always remind myself that the rules that kept me in my place downstairs also kept the people I worked for in their place upstairs – so don't be too hard on them!'

Chapter One

In some houses in the countryside the cook had a lot more to do than cooking. She was expected to kill the chickens, oversee the pig-sticker, deal with the tradesmen and shout at the kitchen maids. I worked in houses where there were several maids to shout at – and sometimes you really did have to shout at the little devils. I also worked where they employed a gardener and a housemaid but no one else, which meant the cook became a bit of a jack of all trades. That's the thing about domestic service; no two houses were the same.

People talk about feeling as if the modern world is split into 'us and them' but they don't know what they're talking about. If you worked as a cook or as any kind of domestic servant when I was young you knew what 'us and them' really meant.

I will give you an example. Even if you worked for the same family for thirty or forty years you were never on first-name terms with them. But, you know, I think servants in many ways felt superior to the people they worked for, particularly later in their careers when they realised that the people who employed them hadn't a clue how to look after themselves. They were like babies!

I remember one woman I worked for – and she was

no duchess I can tell you – used to get all upset when I had my day off or a weekend away. I thought it was because she didn't like being on her own or something but I later found out it was because she didn't know the first thing about cooking. When I was off she had to telephone her friends to ask how to make a cup of tea or boil an egg. I'm not joking. She was too embarrassed to tell me.

The class of person I'm talking about grew up having absolutely everything done for them, so when things got difficult and they couldn't afford servants any longer they got in a terrible state. I found out later that my mistress couldn't even turn the gas stove on.

She had no idea that it was necessary every now and then to take the sheets off the bed and wash them. She'd have slept in them till they stank because all through her life other people had done this for her, so she probably thought it happened by magic!

What was so superior about that? I read a bit about servants when I retired and I realised that things went from one extreme to another over the time I was in service. Up to the 1930s and the Second World War if you didn't work and had no idea how to do anything practical you were considered superior because you could pay someone else to do it all for you – light the fires, wash the clothes and cook the food. By the 1950s it was starting to be embarrassing not to be able to do any of these things. But I only thought about all this much later.

When I was a little girl I lived in a tiny farm worker's cottage on the edge of a small Norfolk village where the local school was expected to send girls up to the big house whenever they were needed – seems a bloody cheek now.

Just because the lady of the manor had a servant sick was that any reason to take another girl away from school? We got little enough education back then anyway.

You have to remember that Norfolk was a very conservative place in the early part of the twentieth century. Things changed very slowly but it also had a bolshie element. The farm workers were often Methodists who left the Church of England because they liked the fact that the Methodists treated everyone as equals. The Church of England still had a system when I was a girl where the local landowners and other bigwigs had their own special pews at the front of the church. The poor people like us were always at the back.

My father was a farm worker, a ploughman mostly, and a Methodist. I remember he told me that at one place where he worked when he was young all the men would shake in their boots when Sir William – the man who owned the estate – wanted to pay a visit to the stables or the yard, which was seldom.

The men would take off their caps and line up and look at the ground. My dad used to say you'd see the younger ones visibly shaking as Sir William walked past. And they daren't look up.

'And he bloody loved it,' my father used to say, meaning that Sir William loved the fact that he could lord it over people whose livelihoods were completely at his disposal.

My father also remembered his baby sister dying because his father, my grandfather, had to walk six miles to fetch the nearest doctor and by the time they got back it was too late. Whole families died from TB and there was malaria still rife in East Anglia and especially on the Fens.

TB was dreaded. We knew a family of six children and slowly over about six or seven years they all died of TB. All of them. I remember how sad it was because one after another the four girls and two boys grew thinner and thinner and then there was a funeral. They were all blond, almost white-haired, and we thought they were beautiful like angels, but they still died. And imagine what it would have been like for their parents who could do nothing and for the children seeing their brothers and sisters die one by one and knowing that it would probably soon be their turn.

I went to see Aggie when she was already ill. As she lay in her dirty little bed she just kept saying to me, 'I don't want to die. I'm scared.' It gave me a very bad opinion of God. But mankind wasn't much better.

My father told me that when he was young farm workers got paid just once a year and if you wanted to leave after six or nine months you got paid nothing at all. So if someone got sick at home or you changed your mind after six months, or the work was too hard, you couldn't say, 'Pay me for what I've done and I'll be off.' No, you lost the lot. By the same token if the farmer felt you weren't up to the job after six months he could send you packing and he didn't have to pay the year's wage. How fair was that?

As a young labourer my father slept in a room with five other farm workers. None of them took their clothes off in six months, he said.

By the time I went into full-time service aged fourteen we were paid each month so that was a bit better. When I got my first proper job, I started as what you'd call a skivvy, I suppose – one of several kitchen maids and really just the scullery maid though we didn't use that word.

Among the female staff there was a lady's maid too, but she was such a superior being we weren't allowed to speak to her and hardly ever saw her.

Chapter Two

It makes me laugh now when I think how the servants in a big house were as status-conscious as their employees. I'll give you an example. In one house where I worked the servants ate at a huge table in the servants' hall. When the housekeeper and the butler had finished eating the first course we all had to stop eating and if you hadn't finished it was hard luck. You had to sit and watch them take your plate away!

It was the same with the main course. You had to watch the top servants and make sure your knife and fork kept up with theirs or your plate would be snatched from under your nose.

They felt they were so far above the lowest servants that they could even dictate the speed at which you ate!

When I met the cook on my first day in my first proper job I thought how grand and important she seemed. I thought I'd like to do that so I quickly made myself useful to her and tried to do as many kitchen jobs as I could and to do them as well as I could.

Mind you, I wouldn't have got to be cook in that big house. It would have taken thirty years to climb that particular ladder, but I moved about a bit more than some and got to be cook in a smaller house.

If I'd known then the long decades I was to spend cooking for other people I think I'd had gone off to America. It wasn't all bad but looking back I realise I used up most of my young life working all the hours God sends so that other people could enjoy a life that involved no work at all.

But it's best to begin at the beginning in that village in Norfolk where I was born in 1907.

We were about thirty miles from Norwich and the city seemed as far away as Paris or New York. It was such a quiet world. No road that I knew round the village was wider than you could spit across and in summer, in the greenest midsummer days, the uncut hedges would almost meet over the narrow roads and we played in these green tunnels and collected wild plums in the hedges.

I'm sure those days before the Great War would have been harsh for my parents, especially in the deep winter, but looking back on my earliest days I can only remember fun and sunshine and all day to play in.

My earliest memory is of the noise of birdsong, so shrill when it had no cars to compete with and when the birds had no chemicals to contend with.

I must have been three or four and toddling in the garden of our cottage where my father grew an amazing variety of vegetables in a tiny space. Most of those vegetables were fertilised by human dung, a thing that wouldn't be allowed now. We must have seemed like medieval peasants and I suppose, in many ways, the things we did were just what a medieval Norfolk peasant would have done.

But really we were just poor and poor people use everything they can and waste nothing.

My father would dig a hole somewhere at the back of the garden about four or five feet deep and he'd move the lean-to till it was above the hole. That lean-to was our lavatory. It was made of wooden planks and had a wooden bench nailed on the inside with a round hole halfway along the bench.

We sat on our poor bare bums on that splintery bench come rain, come shine until the hole in the soil below was starting to fill up a bit. It was never really smelly because the wind came whistling in through the cracks in the boards – and in January when the wind came down across the Norfolk flatlands from Siberia you knew about it, or rather your bum did.

'My arse knows everything there is to know about Russia!' my father used to say.

When you used the toilet you threw a bit of soil on top and that was it – no flushing, no sewage. When the hole was filled to within about eighteen inches or a foot of the surface, Father filled it in with soil and dug another hole and moved the rickety little lean-to again. After twenty years the whole garden was rich in fertiliser and none of us was ever poisoned. We never used any other fertiliser and I tell you those vegetables grew like mad!

I always thought it was similar to the story my mother told me about the village church. She said that centuries before they would gradually fill the churchyard with the dead and then when it was full they would go to the oldest graves, dig up the bones and put them in a room in the basement of the church. This she said was the charnel house.

New bodies could then be buried in the space made by moving the old bones and gradually all the old graves would be emptied until the cycle began again. That way the churchyard space was never used up completely. I saw the charnel house once before it was cleared out – it was filled fifteen feet high with human bones.

My mother loved to tell scary stories like this and I loved the excitement of being scared but only if she hugged me right through the tale.

Chapter Three

Early in the morning and at evening winter and summer we would hear the slow heavy tread of the farm horses. They were massive and my father and the other men rode them sitting sideways, never astride. Don't ask me why but that's what they did and Norfolk was a very conservative place, as I say, so I suppose you'd have been the talk of the village if you aped the gentry and rode astride.

You never trotted the horse either. That would damage its legs and the farmer would be angry. But to a little girl those big horses were giants I dreamed about. The biggest might be seventeen or eighteen hands, weighing a ton or more but so gentle. My father put me up on their backs many times.

Both my parents were storytellers. My father loved to tell the story of the old farm worker who could be heard talking to the plough horse in a loud voice as he rode it home. 'Mind that turn tomorrow on that headland. She's a bugger and no mistake. But we'll see her right won't we? She'll not get the better of thee . . . What did 'ee think of that squall? I know . . . piercing, weren't she? Don't worry your head . . . it'll be better in the morning when we're fresh.' And he'd go on like that till he was out of earshot.

The word 'thee' and other long-dead words were still heard in remote parts of Norfolk before the Great War.

They shot the old horses in the end when they were too old to work and they went to make glue, but the men loved them and hated the tractors when they eventually came in.

Chapter Four

Our cottage was soft red brick, built on a little rise sixty feet from a back road. It was a little damp in winter but not too bad and like many Norfolk farm-workers' cottages it had only the tiniest first floor that you reached using a ladder through a hole in the ceiling – in other words no staircase. The downstairs room had a low wooden ceiling and heavy beams and a red, baked-tile floor.

My father said some of the timbers used for the floorboards and beams were sweet chestnut and always I thought this made us special. Sweet chestnut sounded so lovely.

He once showed me odd holes here and there in the biggest timbers, which were of oak, and he explained that the house had been built from old ships taken apart at Lowestoft a century earlier. He used to say, 'These timbers sailed against Bonaparte and before that the Spanish off Cadiz. How many people live in a house that once sailed the seas and fired on a Spanish galleon?'

There you are you see – stories again.

But I loved that little house and was always happy there and I think my memories of it eventually led to my one great ambition, which was to have a little house of my own, not one owned by the local lord!

My father told many tales but among my childhood favourites was the story of the old monastery on the estate that he had helped demolish back in the late 1890s. I'm sure such a building would have been carefully preserved today but they knocked everything down when I was a child however lovely it was – at least that's what my father said.

Anyway, with their heavy sledgehammers they had broken through a very thick old wall one day and they found themselves in a room about ten feet square and ten high. There were no windows and father said that as he and the other men broke into the room the air was sucked out with a strange noise almost like a sigh.

Everything about the room was odd because not only were there no windows, there was also no sign that there had ever been a doorway into it. With the light coming in as they widened their hole they noticed in one corner a great pile of bundles of firewood each carefully tied up and stacked against the wall.

My father said: 'We went across to them and thought we'd throw them out the hole we'd made before carrying on working. I leant forward and grasped a big solid-looking bundle and my hands just passed through the wood which crumbled to the lightest dust the instant I touched it. That woodpile had probably been there for four hundred years at least.'

I inherited a love of stories from him and it was stories – and a bit of painting – that kept me happy through my long years of domestic service when there was little else to think about.

Despite being a completely uneducated manual worker

my father was clever and always full of interesting facts and fancies.

He had slept on straw as a boy but we slept on flock mattresses and he was proud he'd done so well by us. We had a tiny black range in the downstairs room that we gathered round for heat in winter. It had a little door at the side where there was an oven. It also had a metal plate on top that was always hot.

We had no boiler so there was no hot water on tap, but there was a pump at the back of the cottage that drew up the cold water. You had to work the handle up and down like a mad thing to get the water flowing. My father said that the pipe that went down the hole was made of elm – it was wooden in other words. Isn't that a marvellous thing? And the old metal handle – a massive handle three feet long at least – was made by the local blacksmith. The collar down in the pipe that helped make the vacuum that drew the water up was leather soaked in grease.

You see everything then had still to be made locally because if it was local it was cheap. Imported stuff, even from Norwich just thirty miles away, was expensive.

In summer as a child I'd walk out of the village and see the white dust rising from the still unmade roads. When it had been dry for weeks dust covered everything and we longed for rain. Everyone longed for rain in the spring because Norfolk then, as always, was a dry county and rain was a pleasure for the crops.

I loved the rain because the air smelled clean afterwards and it laid the dust on the roads for a while at least and the sagging plants looked up again. And the farm workers and landowners would relax a bit then too. People didn't celebrate days of sun as they do now.

The ladies – the local gentry ladies I mean – hated the sun because they thought it might brown their skin and that would make them look like the farm girls. They just wanted to be as pale as milk if you please.

Chapter Five

All my childhood, from the earliest day I knew anything, I knew I would have to go into service.

Mother used to say, 'You'll need to know all about kitchen stuff and household things because you'll only be able to live if you can work. You can't live on the parish, you know. And you're a strong girl, you'll do well.'

Strong in those days was a nice way of saying you didn't look a bit like a delicate little princess!

Work was drummed into me and on the longer summer days on the white road where I went out to play a mile or so out from the village there was sometimes a reminder of what happened if you hadn't the money to live and of the shame attached to living on the parish.

Chapter Six

Old workhouse women were paid to pick stones from the field into heaps and these were used on the roads. The women got two bob – two shillings – a ton I think. They had to put the stones in heaps and then the farmer would collect all the stones in a cart and carry them to the road where old men, also from the workhouse, were employed to break the stones into smaller pieces and spread them on the road.

Keeping the roads in a half-decent state was a year-round job because by winter there were always new potholes to fill and if they weren't filled quickly they got deeper and deeper.

I think tar started to come in the late 1920s, but only for the main roads. The tar was heated up in a big iron pot pulled by horses. It was tipped on to the road and then levelled and swept back and forth by men with special brooms.

I remember once an old woman from the workhouse fell down while we watched them work and no one stopped to help her up again. I would have been about six and at first I laughed and then I felt terrible as she just lay there and I ran to get her up. I could see she was in pain and her grey hair had fallen down around her face, which was frightening. She looked like a witch from a storybook.

I helped her back on to her feet and, as any small child would, I kept staring into her face. She suddenly leaned down and said, 'Never mind, missy, never mind,' but she smiled before hobbling back to the stones.

You don't forget these things and in later life whenever I felt fed up with the long hours I had to work I remembered that old woman on the road and it made me save my money in case I should ever have nowhere to turn. Everyone in those days was terrified they'd have nothing in old age and no one had an inkling then that there would be a welfare state and social security.

If you think the countryside was all wandering through the buttercups and gentle milkmaids and sleeping by a sparkling stream you'd be wrong I'm afraid. Don't let anyone tell you the past was better than the modern world. Parts of it were better. I can look back and remember lying by a hedge in summer in a clean white pinafore and listening to the breeze, but through your parents you took in the constant fear of destitution.

My father knew he was completely at the mercy of the local gentry family he worked for. He would always take his hat off if he was working in the garden and a member of the family passed the cottage on a pony or in a carriage. It wasn't so much deference as fear. They had the power of life and death over you. You might have to go at a moment's notice to help out at the big house. My father had to do it now and then if a gardener was sick or if there was no one to fix a gutter.

I can't say we sat around in the evening plotting revolution. My father thought the world would never change and it was better for him now than it had been when he was a child. We had the peasant mentality I suppose. We were fatalistic. We thought it was futile to struggle against the inevitable. The extent to which we were afraid is hard to imagine in the modern world where everyone has rights.

I remember my mother once suggesting we put up a picture on the wall of our downstairs room, but my father told her not to do it in case it damaged the wall and we were turfed out as a result.

And this was in a cottage that probably cost five pounds to put up; a cottage with three rooms each measuring about ten foot square and covered in rough old plaster. You could see the horsehair sticking through it.

Chapter Seven

The countryside before the First World War was a place as different from the modern world as it is possible to imagine. No one speaks now as we did then. The local accent was so strong that people from Norfolk would only half understand people from other parts of the country or they wouldn't understand them at all.

An uncle of mine went once to Romney Marsh in Kent to bring some sheep home and he marvelled at the fact that he could barely understand a word anyone said. As far as his Norfolk neighbours were concerned he was as good as Marco Polo because it was so rare for us to go anywhere. He seemed a real adventurer just for going to Kent.

And our isolation led to strange goings-on. There was a house about half a mile from us, a lonely house in an orchard that you could only reach across a field. There was no road to it at all. Here a brother and sister lived with six children.

Now, no one said a word at the time in public but it was common knowledge that those children's parents were the brother and sister. They were a funny family in every way; kept themselves close to themselves as many people did back then. Pretended they weren't in when anyone called. Cottagers weren't sociable in the way they are portrayed in books about the old countryside that make it seem so golden and rosy.

In the village there were always jealousies that this family was getting above itself or that family were slovens that respectable people should have nothing to do with. Village life was so narrow that we couldn't take the broader view because hardly anyone had been more than twenty miles in any direction.

We thought the whole world was like where we were.

Chapter Eight

Early childhood spares you the deeper meaning and the sadness of these things. That comes later and, besides, my father and mother were kind to me and I felt safe and secure. This is a great thing if your later life is going to be hard.

I could play in the garden and wander the lanes. Not far off was a stream we dammed, the other village children and I, and we tried to catch the small fish in our hands. We made little dens in the thick hedges – hedges that were later to be cut down by nasty, smoky flailing machines.

In my childhood the hedges were allowed to grow up because they could not easily be cut by hand, a back-breaking and slow task. But wasn't that great for the birds which were everywhere? And for the children, of course.

There were no bought toys I recall, only whistles we made from reed stems and a few games.

I was an only child, which was unusual then, but a good thing as farm workers earned so little, and so I probably had more than the children in big families. I don't remember minding a bit that I had no brothers and sisters because my parents always seemed interesting to me. My father could write his own name and very slowly write a simple letter but he'd more or less taught himself, having never been to school.

He loved it when I drew – drawing was my favourite pastime – and despite the fact that we had little money he managed to buy me coloured chalks and paper. Heaven knows where he got them but they gave me a taste for drawing and painting that stayed with me for life.

My father had started work as a boy milking cows on a small farm and was paid about a farthing for two cows, or that's what he used to say. I loved listening to him on Sunday – the only day he wasn't too tired to talk.

He used to tell me then about domestic service as a step up from his life. I think he thought that because my mother had been a maid and had happy memories of it. She'd told him about the silver and the china and glasses and it had a romantic air I suppose. Father thought I'd be in big houses among grand, educated people. I don't think it really occurred to him that I'd be working night and day and looked down on. He thought I'd be indoors in the warmth and not out in the fields in the rain with an old sack over my shoulders as he had been since childhood.

Poor country people could only look up so far. The idea that I might have a job at a desk and a house of my own was beyond him. But from the time I could think about anything at all I wanted my own cottage that no one could ever take away. That was my great ambition.

Most of the boys went into farming and most of the girls went into service because all around were big farms, even bigger country houses and, in Norwich, plenty of big town houses. Anyone with even a moderate income could afford a skivvy or two.

My father hated the town. I loved to hear the story of

his life because it went back well into the nineteenth century. From the age of about ten he had got to know the farm horses. He became what was known as the yard lad on the estate and had to be up at six feeding them. He'd then muck out the stables ready for when they were back from the fields.

He told me that by the age of sixteen he'd learned to plough a two-horse team by following an experienced man up the fields and in the evenings he'd lead the horses through the farm pond to get the heavy clay off their feet. If you left it on them, he said, they'd soon catch a sort of foot rot we called 'farsy'.

I remember him saying there were four horses and four men to every one hundred acres of land when he was a boy. That's a lot of men and horses, but even in my childhood the countryside was still a busy place, much busier than it was by the 1960s and 1970s, because farming had hardly any machinery and most jobs were still done by hand.

My father loved the horses and he loved telling us about them. He'd describe them trembling and blowing with exhaustion as they pulled the plough up the heavy clay soils. When they stopped he'd hack the great clouts of mud from their legs while they nuzzled him. He'd say that a man had to walk fourteen miles with his horses to plough one acre, which is roughly what could be done in a day.

Imagine doing that every day for weeks, then years on end.

Chapter Nine

Farm workers and their families never took holidays. We had no spare money and where could we go? But we had games. By candles and oil lamps we played dominoes and draughts. Only the big houses round about had gas lamps, often from gas they generated themselves using a special carbide generator – this was a way of mixing calcium carbide with water to create a gas you could burn.

The cottagers had just a big old fire and a few candles, or oil lamps later on, but I don't remember being particularly uncomfortable. You had to go to bed early anyway, in order to be up early.

My father, but never mother, went now and then to the pub which was about a mile away. I remember going in once to call my father. That was the only time I saw inside one.

All country pubs looked more or less the same inside in those days. A big fire, a few scrubbed deal tables and a few old boys sitting round with their mugs of beer and smoking hard. Everyone smoked short clay pipes for all they were worth. In our village when a man went in the pub the first thing the landlord did was to give him a pipe because clay pipes were cheap then.

My father hated a new pipe so when the landlord gave him one he'd straight away give it to another old boy till it had been smoked black, then my father would have it back. He liked them well worn in.

People were very rough, particularly when they'd had a few drinks. The worst offence my father said was to pick up another man's beer. You might easily do it, too, if you'd had a few and were a bit merry, but if you did there was a very good chance he'd knock you down for it without a word.

And some old country boys just liked getting into fights for the fun of it, or so my father said.

Chapter Ten

Even horse traffic was scarce in the twenties. You could drive a cart for miles and you'd rarely pass another. Most people walked everywhere. My mum and dad didn't even have a bicycle and only people with a lot of money could afford a pony and trap. In his whole life my father only went as far as Norwich, though occasionally he'd borrow a cart to carry something for himself or someone in the village.

There were different horses kept for the different forms of transport: hackneys were for riding and showing, ponies pulled traps and small carts and, of course, there were ordinary carthorses for the heavy wagons and for ploughing.

I remember the pub stables lined with horses or they'd be tied up in the street at rings fixed in the brickwork of the wall. No one we knew rode a horse around the place. That was something only the quality could afford because you needed a saddle, a bridle and a proper riding horse, a hackney, which would cost a great deal more than a pony or a carthorse. It just wasn't for the likes of us so we didn't aspire to it.

Funny things happened around the farm stables. I heard that a terrier that ran about the yard lived almost entirely on testicles – it was always there when the young horses were being gelded and as soon as the knot was tied and the testicles cut off the terrier would jump on them and swallow them whole. It would do it with the sheep too. It had a sixth sense about where to be at the right time!

The great game played by all the men and boys in those days, but watched by some of the girls on a Saturday afternoon, was quoits. Matches were always played in the pub yard. A quoit is a ring of iron weighing as much as eleven pounds. An iron peg with a feather stuck in it was driven into the centre of the quoit bed, which was a clay area designed to make the quoits stick. No money was ever bet on a game but a gallon or two of beer might go to the winner of a game and the loser bought the beer. You had to throw your quoits eighteen yards and each man had two quoits. Four men would play at any one tie.

Like horses quoits just seemed to reach the end of its days and it disappeared completely in the 1950s, despite the fact that the men all over Norfolk had loved it.

You see once again – only the men. Norfolk was so conservative that women such as my mother lived as women had lived for centuries: they looked after the children and the house and gossiped and never went anywhere or did anything much beyond cook and clean.

Chapter Eleven

I think old people had the worst of it when I was young. I lived into an age when the government would give you enough to live on if you had nothing, but when I was a child the elderly might easily starve if they had no one to look after them.

I remember old Nat Budgen who lived in the next village from us in the filthiest little cottage you've ever seen. He got up with the dawn and went to bed at sunset, never owned a clock and had no idea of the time. Nat had lived alone from the time his parents died, according to my father. One winter afternoon my father went over to see if the old boy was all right and found him dead in his bed and half eaten by animals that had got in by the broken windows and door. He had probably grown weak from lack of food and then the cold killed him. That sort of death wasn't uncommon before the Great War.

Neighbours might help, of course, but you could still easily end up in the workhouse and many would rather die in a ditch than that. It was also hard for women if they had husbands who spent all their wages in the pub. And many did, while their wives struggled to bring up twelve or thirteen children in a tiny cottage without heat or light or water.

On the other hand I do miss some of the old characters who lived round about. There were marvellous eccentrics who did as they pleased despite all the rules imposed on us in those days.

In my last years of freedom before I started as a domestic servant, I used to walk a mile and a half on a Sunday to see Mrs Patey, an old woman who all the children round about loved. She was one of those people who was so delighted to have a visitor that she made you feel really special. She was the complete opposite of the mad old cottagers who hid themselves away and distrusted everyone.

Mrs Patey would almost run down the path of her cottage to catch hold of you and bring you into her little sitting room. I remember a few days after my tenth birthday I'd gone to see her just for something to do. I hadn't seen her for a few weeks and many other children called in regularly because she almost always gave us sweets or bread and jam and made a fuss of us. When I walked up her path she appeared at the doorway and shouted: 'It's the birthday girl. Oh, I'm so pleased you've come. I've made you a little cake and a present.'

I had no memory of mentioning my coming birthday to her but I suppose I must have or she perhaps just knew about it because she made it her business to know. Children were her great love and her hobby really.

So I sat on her big old sofa smiling my head off while she bustled about in the kitchen saying every now and then, 'Oh I'm so pleased you've come. I really am. I'm so pleased.'

She made me a little cup of tea with lots of sugar and then appeared with a small cake beautifully iced and gave it to me. I don't think she'd made it especially for me at all because she always had plenty of cakes ready for anyone who called, but it was so sweet of her. It's as clear now to me as if it happened yesterday.

The cake was delicious and while I ate it she said she'd made my tea in a cup and saucer because now I was a lady. How that made me laugh when I thought about it in later years! I must have seen Mrs Patey at least once a month or more for the whole time I was growing up and before I went into service and I never remember her being the least out of temper, even when three or four children were already on her sofa eating her out of house and home.

Her sitting room was like a mad junk shop where you could never be bored. She had half a dozen or more grandfather clocks of various sizes, none of which worked, two pigeons in a cage – 'They're Norfolk love-birds,' she used to say – and more cats than you could count.

When I was about to leave to live in as a servant I went to see her and gave her the news. It was the only time I saw her look sad. 'I do hope they will be kind to you,' she said. But she knew, as I did, that for country girls childhood came to an early end.

Chapter Twelve

When I was a girl all the women wore ankle-length dresses and leather button-up boots. It was all so bloomin' impractical, especially when you went into service, because long dresses and petticoats got in the way and made you so hot in summer when you were already in a baking hot kitchen. Trousers would have been much better, but I don't think a single woman in the country wore trousers then. You'd have been arrested or stoned to death!

And it wasn't much better for the men. Farm workers such as my father always wore hobnailed boots made of the thickest leather. If the boots got soaked they'd be iron hard the next morning when they came to put them on. And tough though those boots were they would generally last only a year. Most ordinary men would have only one pair of boots at a time and no other shoes at all. A pair of boots might cost 10 shillings and I reckon every working man in Norfolk wore the same sort, bloody great things with nails driven into the soles.

I ran around with no boots at all until I was about three and then had a second-hand pair my mother got from heaven knows where. I remember seeing older children running about winter and summer with nothing on their feet.

Though women were mostly kept at home they still helped with the harvest and we children went out to the fields winter and summer when we felt like it if we hadn't yet gone to school. Some days I stayed at home to help Mother, other days I was free just to wander. Mother used to say, 'Enjoy yourself while you can, you'll not be young forever,' which was a view some mothers didn't have. Other girls round about were kept at it every day with little tasks round the house from the time they were four or five.

I was a very pretty little girl with very dark eyes and lots of dark brown curls, but too skinny according to my mother. The idea of me ever being skinny seemed ridiculous later on because I turned into a stout young woman but very strong and with hair that I had to wrestle into a bun or under a hat.

As a little girl I loved to go about with my father who always smiled and said yes when I asked if I could go with him round the farm. I persuaded him one time to let me go with him to cart manure out to the fields although that was a terrible job because the muck was spread by hand and Father always came back smelling terrible.

Barley and hay and corn were often still cut by hand at this time. It was all done with scythes as it had been done for as long as anyone could remember. And when the hay was brought in from the fields the children would climb high up on the wagon – maybe ten feet up on the hay – for the journey to the farmyard where the hay was unloaded. They were happy days because it was summer and nothing is as sweet as good cut hay. And then the hayricks were a marvel to see. They were roughly ten yards by five yards – the height of a twenty-stave ladder – and they'd have a thatched roof just like a house.

So this was the world I knew, but all the time I was growing I knew that there would be no choice about what I would do when I left school. Poor girls didn't work on the land. They went into service.

I'd mostly be working indoors, I knew, and as my parents told me how much better that would be than working in the fields I came to accept it and even looked forward to it. I thought I'd be in the city, perhaps, with the bright lights or at least be with other girls and make friends. I never thought much about the work itself.

Chapter Thirteen

Things began to change as I grew towards my teens. My days wandering the fields were fewer now and my mother asked me to do more around the house.

Years later she told me it was deliberate because she knew that when I was fourteen or fifteen I would have to start work. They just couldn't afford to keep me any longer. Isn't it odd that people had children then – and usually loads of them – when they knew they couldn't afford to keep them beyond thirteen or fourteen?

I often wondered why people had so many children if they were all destined to be slaves. Part of the reason was that there was no way to stop having children and another was that a man was expected to have children when he married in case people thought he wasn't a real man. No one thought about whether they could afford to keep a whole brood.

Some families probably thought a bit more about it and perhaps thought they'd have someone to look after them in their old age, but no poor families I ever heard of in our rural part of Norfolk would keep a child on at school beyond fourteen or fifteen. They pushed them out in the world and they were expected to contribute to the family budget by sending money home if they were away in service or handing it over if they were boys and went to work on the local estate with their fathers.

So when I was about eight I started to do more than a few simple chores. I watched Mother make pies from apples from our tree and from local honey. I went with her to the nearest shop which was a mile away and I saw how carefully she bought things – only things we couldn't grow ourselves of course: flour, tea and so on. We always had a pig fattening for Christmas and that, along with a few pigeons and an occasional chicken, was pretty much all the meat we ever had. Some of the pig was sold after it was killed and we ate some fresh at Christmas and the rest smoked and salted.

I felt sorry for the pigs. They'd become quite tame as they grew and grunted with delight when they saw you coming with the slop bucket.

Then came the time for the pig-sticker and you'd hear the screams of the pig a mile away when the poor thing was dragged out of its little pen and hit on the head with a great blunt hammer. I think they had an inkling what was coming, but sometimes the sticker would be a kind man and give the pig a bowl of bran that it would be eating when it was hit. That way it was probably happy at the last moment and not terrified. I had to hold a basin under the pig's throat to catch the blood after its jugular was cut and I remember watching the heart still pumping like mad but of course it was pumping the pig's life away.

I began to learn to cook by chopping vegetables, fetching water for Mother, rolling out the pastry and collecting apples and other fruit and vegetables from the garden. I had to do housework too but I always knew I would hate housework when I went into service because working in a kitchen always seemed a much better option – you might have to make things for other people to eat but at least you were making things for them rather than cleaning up their mess.

As my mother had been in service before she got married, she explained to me that I would have to start at the bottom, but perhaps to protect me she didn't tell me the hours I'd have to work or the strict ways of a kitchen in a big house or the odd characters I might have to put up with! I suppose she wanted to make it sound exciting so that when the time came I wasn't afraid to go.

Chapter Fourteen

I was lucky because elementary school was free so I could go and loved going, from the age of five. I walked across the fields to the local school, which was in the next village. The school had just two small rooms. Juniors were in one end with the male teacher and infants in the other with the female teacher. Each classroom had a fire and the fires were back to back. By that I mean there was a massive central chimney stack with a fire on both sides – one for the mistress and one for the master.

The fires were right behind where the teachers stood at the front of the class so they got the greatest benefit in winter and the children vied for places near the front on cold days because the back of the classroom was like an ice house.

We had to take a few lumps of coal or collect sticks when we walked to school in winter and you were in trouble if you turned up empty-handed. I can recall a little boy who came from an outlying hamlet hopping through the snow with a great load of sticks in an old sack and another boy turned up with some dried horse dung that they burned at home but the master wouldn't use because of the smell. The poor boy's parents clearly couldn't afford logs or coal or the boy might have been simple-minded and thought he could bring anything – I never found out.

Most girls were very well behaved at school but the boys were sometimes little devils. They were often hit by the teacher and some days you'd hear the teachers on both sides of the chimney shouting fit to bust and then walking around belting the kids. The children would often go home covered with bruises and their parents, seeing the bruises, would beat them some more, knowing that they'd been in trouble at school.

The teachers were quite eccentric too. Mr Robertson, who taught the older children, used to shout to his wife now and then, 'Are you ready for tea, missus?' or, 'Is the blasted Biggs boy with you?' and as they left the connecting door between the two classrooms open Mrs Robertson would just shout a reply. Sometimes they'd carry on a whole conversation like this in tandem. Sometimes they'd combine a conversation with shouting at us about the capital cities of Europe or the times table.

He'd say, 'How's Mrs Firkin's dropsy? . . . What's eight times four?'

She'd reply, 'She's a lot better since that devil Eric left . . . What's the capital of Egypt?'

There was a boy in my class who could hardly do anything and he was allowed to just sit chewing paper or staring out the window. He never did any work because he just couldn't and everyone knew it but mostly we were all kind to him or at least left him alone and of course there was no provision then for children who couldn't learn. They were just referred to as being a bit simple. It was the same with adults.

Every district had one or two old boys, simpletons who wandered the lanes and slept in ditches. They'd disappear now and then, sometimes for months, and then just as suddenly reappear.

Chapter Fifteen

I remember The Piper, an old man who used to call at all the cottages round about asking for food and money or sometimes just for tea. He might have been simple but he was canny in some ways because he never turned up too often and had a way you'd almost describe as charming.

He was called The Piper because he always carried a penny whistle which he played really well.

If Mother was a bit cross with him he'd jump back immediately and whip out the tin whistle and stay playing like mad. I loved it so I used to say to my mother when it might be him at the door, 'Don't be too nice to him or he won't play!' He once told me he'd walked to Paris and played outside Notre Dame. I don't know if it was true but he always vanished in the worst winter months, probably to London.

The only other people we saw were gypsies who still came along through the lanes now and then in brightly covered horse-drawn wagons. They were very clever and made beautiful things from hedge timber but the local people hated them. My mother, who was a tolerant soul most of the time, called them devils from the east. I was caught in the lane once when one of them shouted to me from their little camp.

I went across nervously, because children tend to do as they are asked even if they are very unsure about whatever it is. I might have been nine or ten I think and they sat me down and asked a little about the village and my parents and they gave me a tiny cup of something very hot and sweet to drink. It tasted of earth but pleasant. After a minute or two I found I was chatting away to them as if they were my best friends. The old woman among them sat on the step of their wagon and I remember her face was like leather, tanned almost black, and she wore her hair in two braids down either side of her face which seemed strange to me as she was so old. The women in the village who were old never cut their hair – in fact no woman ever cut her hair – but they always wore it up.

But the gypsies that day had a way of making you feel at home and I remembered they all smelled of woodsmoke, a very sweet smell and not unpleasant at all.

When I suddenly remembered who they were and where I was I hopped up feeling guilty and said I had to go home. They gave me a small wooden dog so beautifully carved that I thought it must have been bought in a shop. But later I was told gypsies never bought anything in shops. I was worried that my parents might think I had stolen the wooden dog. In fact they were bound to be very suspicious and I knew they'd be furious if I told them I'd been talking to gypsies, so I hid the dog in a hedge and into my old age I can still remember the bitter regret when, the next morning, I went back to the hedge and the dog had gone.

I hunted all along thinking I might have forgotten where exactly I'd put it but I could never find it. Since then I've always loved the gypsies – although when I saw the horrible modern caravans they used after the Second World War I was sad that they could leave behind all the things that made them so special.

One other thing that little band of gypsies showed me before I ran off home was cooking, but not the sort of cooking I was later to do myself!

I'd been watching a girl on the outskirts of the group for some time. She was sitting by a small fire and poking about in it. She was the one who gave me the hot sweet root drink and now I saw her take something from the fire. It looked like a mud ball – about the size of a football. She brought it over to the others in a thick bit of dirty cloth.

She crouched down and hit the clay with a small piece of iron and it cracked in two. Inside was what looked a bit like a chicken. It steamed and smelled quite good to me, although I hoped they wouldn't offer me any as I hated the idea of eating with people I didn't know.

As I looked the girl broke off the pieces of meat and put them on a tin plate. It was then that I noticed the spines embedded in the thick clay she'd broken to get at the meat. They were hedgehog spines and their clever trick of cooking ensured that the animal could be cooked whole but when they wanted to eat it the spines would come off with the baked clay.

All the time I sat with them they smiled and talked and I noticed a very beautiful little boy among the children who had a song thrush on one shoulder. It wasn't on a string or anything and hadn't had its wings clipped. Every now and then the boy fed it a tidbit and it sang away quite contentedly. I was dazzled and later remembered the gypsies' reputation for taming horses and domesticating all sorts of difficult animals.

I never forgot my encounter with the gypsies. I went back the next day when I couldn't find my dog but they had gone and only the embers of their fire were left.

Chapter Sixteen

The nearest big house to us was owned by a farmer who employed a maid of all work. Well, I was told he employed her but it turned out that she hardly ever turned up and when she did she used to shout at him and tell him off. It was said that she came and went as she pleased and she was thought to be a little mad by everyone round about, so I think he must have liked being scolded by her.

The farmer lived in what seemed like a big house to us. It was certainly big in comparison to our little cottage. It had four or five bedrooms so it seemed huge to me, but there was nothing grand about it.

The farmer brewed his own beer, grew his own tobacco and vegetables and reared all his own meat, although it was rumoured that what he mostly ate was rabbits he caught or shot himself.

All the locals and most of the boys set traps for rabbits then – usually a bit of wire tied into a free-running noose and then held down by a small wooden stake driven into the ground. They'd set it low down on a known rabbit run and next morning they'd usually have a rabbit. Many mornings I heard the scream of a trapped rabbit and sometimes the wire would catch only one leg and they'd pull and pull until the wire cut through to the bone.

If the trap wasn't checked it might take several days for the poor rabbit to die, but no one cared about that sort of thing then. It was the same with foxes, which the gamekeepers were told to destroy by any means – unless there was a local hunt in which case the keeper would be sacked if he touched a fox. If a fox was caught by the leg in a wire it would sometimes chew its own leg off to escape.

That old farmer gave me my first job. Not my first proper job but it was domestic work. I was about twelve, nearly thirteen I think, and what a rum one he turned out to be. I think he must have met my mother going along the road or something because she suddenly said to me one day while we were working together in the kitchen, 'Nancy, Mr Mayes needs a help on Saturdays. He'll give you sixpence for an afternoon so get off there this Saturday.'

You didn't argue with your parents back then so I just said I'd go.

'What does he want me for?' I asked.

'Oh, just to feed the chickens and wash and clean and cook a bit. I don't really know – a bit of help with all things but it will be good for you to learn something before you get a proper job.'

The following Saturday I set off for Mr Mayes' farm, which was about a mile and a half away. I'd probably seen old Mayes' farm many times before and never paid much heed to it, but on that Saturday afternoon I noticed every detail. It stood close to the road where the road took a sharp bend. It was a crooked old house with a roof that went up and down like a camel's back and tiny windows set in plaster walls.

Here and there, visible between the white areas of plaster, were huge grey wooden beams. They weren't painted fashionable black as they would be much later. They were just left to weather and looked a sort of steely grey. There was a massive chimney stack rising out of the centre of the house so that the whole building looked like it hung from the chimney. The chimneys themselves were twisted like sticks of barley sugar. The garden at the front of the house was overgrown and the short brick path to the front door had weeds coming up through it.

I was a slight thing then, not the sturdy creature I later became. I remember noticing how thin my hand looked when I nervously lifted it up to knock on the door. Ridiculous really, but I was worried I'd knock too loud so I started with a gentle tap. My knuckles bounced soundlessly off the great grey planks of the massive door. There was no iron knocker and no string or wire for a bell. I stood for a while feeling silly, tapped a bit louder and then set off round the side of the house. I had to push my way through weeds and plants that had grown high up against the side of the house.

None of this surprised me because few people except the gentry had time to keep their houses looking spick and span with well-tended gardens. Mr Mayes was better off by far than we were but he wasn't gentry.

From the back of the house I could hear a thumping noise so I gradually made my way around the overgrown garden path. I saw Mr Mayes at last. There he was, fat like Mr bloomin' Pickwick. I'd say he was about fifty then with a very red face and no hair at all on his head and a dirty grey beard and no moustache. When I got the chance to estimate them, I realised he had about four teeth left in his crooked mouth.

He smiled broadly like a gargoyle and said, 'You must be Nancy. I've been looking forward to you coming. You'll like it here, oh yes.' And he sort of leered at me and laughed to himself. I found I couldn't get a word out to reply because in addition to his terrible red face and lack of teeth I then noticed for the first time that he was wearing a home-made rabbit fur scarf and I could still see the rabbit's ears on it and the holes where its eyes had been.

When I recovered from the shock I told him I was Nancy, which was pretty bloody obvious, and he asked me to follow him into the house.

We went through a passageway that ran straight through the middle of the house from back to front and sort of around one side of the enormous central chimney stack. There were big red tiles on the floor but many were missing and underneath it was just bare earth. The walls on either side of the passage were made of massive planks slotted into huge upright timbers – no plaster here at all.

That showed what an old house it was. The inside probably hadn't been altered or modernised at all since the house was built. This made the passageway very dark even though the door at the back that we'd come through was wide open and it was a bright sunny day.

Halfway along the corridor I followed him into a big room which had a few chairs, a sofa and one of those massive fireplaces that seem to take up half the room. All the floor tiles were missing here and old Mayes' furniture sat on crooked hammered earth. There was a low fire smouldering in the big fireplace and the room smelled damp and smoky. All big fires smoked into the room in those days because they drew so badly, but like most country people who had open fires Mr Mayes wasn't in the least bit bothered. He was also expert at pretty much never letting it go out. The trick was to cover the flames with just the right amount of ash when you went to bed so that the embers would stay alive and then a few dried twigs would get the thing going in the morning.

I stood there feeling a little awkward while he searched around on top of a table and then in a cupboard. He sort of growled and grumbled while he did it. All I heard was, 'Come on out of it, grrr, where are you, you beggar . . . grrr . . .' and all the while he rummaged and dug impatiently through piles of stuff I couldn't really see.

Then he stopped, lifted up a key and then beckoned me out into the back garden again. I followed him to the end of the garden and he pointed to a green-painted shed and said, 'That's the privy and this is the key for it. I'll hang it on a hook just inside the back door. Here it is so you'll recognise it.'

Well I thought that was the funniest thing ever — fancy the first thing he thought I'd need to know was the whereabouts of the lav! And I'd never heard of anyone locking their lav either. I mean, what did he keep in there?

After that he gave me a broom and said I was to sweep the yard at the back and then he wanted me to cook his supper and to make enough for two days. After I swept the yard I swept inside the house but because of the earth floors I think I kicked up more dust than I moved.

His kitchen was the big room on the other side of the central passage from the sitting room where we'd been earlier. As I worked with the brush he came in every now and then and said, 'Very good, very good,' but he was an odd man who'd look at you sideways the whole time with his squinty blue eyes and then stand too close to you when he was speaking. No wonder he was a bachelor. He'd left a few onions and carrots and potatoes on the kitchen table and he said, 'I want chicken. You can kill any chicken you like – they're in a run away at the back from the house.'

Well, this was a pretty pickle. I'd never killed anything and here I was expected to wring one of the poor creatures' necks. I slowly chopped the onion and the potatoes thinking I'd just make a big pot of stew like I'd done many times with my mother at home. But I couldn't bring myself to go and get the chicken or to tell him I was afraid to do it. Eventually he came back in and I said, 'I can't kill the chicken. I've never done it.'

He just laughed and went straight out. A few minutes later he was back with a dead bird which he threw down on the table.

'I suppose you know how to pluck it?' he said. I told him I knew because I'd seen my mother do it, although that was usually with pigeons the local keeper had shot and given to my dad. We hardly ever had chicken. I was amazed at how warm and soft that bird was but it took me nearly an hour to pluck while the vegetables simmered on the range.

The thing about plucking is that you have to do it carefully because no one likes the skin to be broken – I found out about that much later when I worked in big houses. There's a trick to doing it quickly and carefully but it takes time to learn.

Anyway I didn't pluck that first one all that well but I didn't think the old man would notice. Drawing the bird – gutting it I mean – was much worse. I cut it up as best I could and dropped the pieces into the pot with the bits of carrot, potato, cabbage and onion. It was my first masterpiece as a cook! Then I froze. I realised I'd forgotten to fry the chicken first, but the house seemed such a mess and he seemed such a ramshackle old so-and-so that I thought if it was well cooked he wouldn't notice.

His range was much bigger than ours with two ovens with big heavy latches on their doors. There was also a bread oven built into the brickwork at the side. It all looked very complicated to me but it had been well lit and was good and hot so I stuffed the pot in, shut the door and hoped for the best.

I was about to go out and see what he wanted next because I could hear him in the garden but I thought I'd have a little look round first. Apart from the big table and a few cupboards, there wasn't much in that kitchen, I can tell you. Two oil lamps threw out a miserly bit of light so that despite the bright afternoon the room was dark. There was a big old clock that didn't work, a massive old oak sideboard with the date 1680 on it that reached almost to the ceiling, and a few rickety chairs.

I expect Mayes' family had been there for centuries because no one bought furniture then, not a small farmer like Mr Mayes anyway, and it was all so old you just knew it had come to him with the house. His stuff would have been worth a lot by the time I was an old woman but back then it was just out-of-date heavy furniture – the sort of furniture that I saw thrown out in the 1950s and 1960s when people hated that sort of thing.

So it was a gloomy house but I remember it well because my work for Mr Mayes and the bit of cooking I'd done with my mother were really the start of my career as a cook. I knew on that first day that I would always prefer cooking to sweeping up – and that was true even taking into account the poor chicken!

It was good to get back out of the gloom into the sun even if I did have to talk to Mr Mayes again. I found him digging a hole under a tree and he stopped and looked up at me. He was pouring with sweat and his rabbit scarf had been stuffed into his shirt so he looked as if he had no neck. He wiped his face with his hand, reached into his waistcoat pocket and pulled out a sixpence and gave it to me. 'See you next Saturday,' he said. 'Come at dinner time' – that meant lunchtime back then. Off I went then as fast as my legs would carry me.

Well the days went by and the following Saturday came around and I walked back to Mr Mayes' farmhouse again. This time he was in his big sitting room poking about in the fire.

He didn't bother to say good morning or even hello. He just said, 'Can you read?'

I was very proud of my reading so I couldn't help boasting. 'I'm almost the best in my class,' I blurted out and then blushed.

'Good,' he said and gave me a list.

On it were all the things he wanted me to do that day. It seemed a huge amount to me but it was nothing to the work I would later do when I worked full time in service.

My first job was to wash up a week's worth of plates. He had a typical bachelor's kitchen, or at least that's how I thought of it later. Very messy and dirty and most of the old plates and cups were cracked and chipped. None of it bothered him in the slightest.

I boiled a kettle and filled the kitchen sink as best I could before trying to get the muck off the plates and pots. One thing I noticed was that he'd used the plates several times each without cleaning them. So although there weren't too many it was murder to get the grease off. The germs on those plates after being reused for a week don't bear thinking about.

Mayes had one massive bar of soap that he used for everything – washing himself, washing the floors and washing the plates, so I had to use that. It was all a bit disgusting but living in the country back then you got used to dirt and mess, although my mother was organised and orderly and scrupulous about cleanliness.

The other things on my list were to collect beans from the garden and dig up a few potatoes, pluck the two pigeons he'd left lying on the kitchen table, sweep upstairs and wash the upstairs floors. For such a grubby old man he was funny about washing the floors – they were bare wood in the bedrooms that were hardly ever used but every other Saturday he'd ask me to wash them down.

The weeks went by like this and I continued at school and earned my sixpence each Saturday from Mr Mayes. Then one Saturday there was a shift in the way he behaved. He'd never been nice about my work. He'd never made a fuss and said what I'd cooked him was any good or that I'd worked hard and the kitchen or sitting room looked nice. I just accepted that that was the way

63

he was. He never ever noticed when I picked a few flowers from the garden and left them in a bottle on the kitchen table. I'd also improved my cooking over the months with a little help from my mother. He always wanted stews of one kind or another – pigeon or rabbit or chicken – and my mother told me what to add to vary it a bit; a few herbs, a bit of pepper, that sort of thing.

But old Mayes never commented on any of this. On the other hand he never complained either.

Then, as I say, it all changed. It was about six months after I started my Saturdays with him.

I told him I was leaving school soon – I was fourteen by now and I said that I would probably be getting a full-time job somewhere in service. He didn't say a word at the time but I noticed a bit later that he looked grumpy and when I asked him a question he scowled and didn't reply. He improved a bit over the coming weeks but was never as friendly as he had been when I started. Mind you, that wasn't saying much! Then shortly after I stopped going to school my mother took me aside and said, 'Mr Mayes has asked you to work for him full time.'

Well, I didn't like the sound of that but what could I say? I knew I would be working full time now I was no longer at school and perhaps it might as well be at Mr Mayes' as anywhere else. And at least I'd be coming home every night.

I'd been giving my sixpence each week to my mother. She'd given me a penny or two now and then for my piggy bank so with a full time job now I'd have a bit more money.

But how I would have loved to carry on at school. It felt such a wrench, but only the local gentry children went to school in Ipswich or Norwich and you needed money for that. Money we didn't have.

'Doesn't Mr Mayes already have someone else in the week?' I asked my mother.

'She's gone,' said my mother.

So it was settled.

Chapter Seventeen

A week later I set off for the farm thinking, I'm grown-up now and this is a real job, although of course it wasn't anything of the sort. Mr Mayes had agreed to pay my mother direct. I didn't mind as you were brought up then to think that your duty was to the family not yourself and I'd still be a burden on my parents as I'd be going home every night. I was to eat at Mr Mayes' in the daytime, at breakfast and dinner.

Mr Mayes was pretty much grumpy all the time now. He looked at me strangely when I arrived and stomped off upstairs after a couple of minutes. I knew the ropes by now so I cleaned the sitting room and kitchen as best I could and then set off to murder a chicken as that was about the only thing Mayes had told me to do.

I'd lost my terror of killing things but it still wasn't a nice thing to have to do. Chickens are funny creatures. They make a huge fuss as you try to grab them, flapping and rushing about and squawking, but once you have them in your hands they calm down completely.

Many people would kill them by putting the head on a block and cutting it off with the little hand-axe kept for splitting logs. I'd seen people do it like this but it was

67

messy and if you let go of the bird afterwards you got blood everywhere as it then thrashed around.

Other people used to pull the chicken's head till the neck broke but there was an art to that and you might give it a terrific pull only to find that the bird was perfectly alive still and blinking and looking at you accusingly. I'd also seen people holding a chicken by the head and spinning its body around hoping that the neck would eventually break. That hardly ever worked.

All this sort of thing was an everyday part of country life then and few worried about animal suffering. I was just a bit squeamish so I used a small club that Mr Mayes kept on a nail by the chicken shed. He'd shown me how to use it. It was like a policeman's truncheon but weighted with lead at one end. If you hit the chicken hard on the back of the head – and mind it did have to be hard – it would knock it senseless and you could then hit it again, but all these methods could be messy and I sometimes missed with the club and ended up swiping at it a few times.

The only thing I used to say to myself was that I hoped God wasn't a big chicken or we'd all be in a lot of trouble later on.

Now I was working every day except Sunday for Mr Mayes I quickly found the job boring because I was cleaning the same few rooms every day and cooking the same few stews he liked day in and day out. I asked my mother if I could maybe change jobs but she said no. I think she liked to have me coming home each evening and Mayes was paying her quite well for my help.

After a few months during which there were no mishaps I dropped and broke a mixing bowl. Mayes was furious. It was bad luck that he happened to be in the kitchen at the time so he saw it as it happened. What happened next gave me the biggest shock of my life. He immediately grabbed me, put me over his knee and hit me really hard half a dozen times with the flat of his hand on my bottom. When he'd finished he pushed me off his lap and walked straight out without a word or a look. I was so shocked that I went back to my work and only after about ten minutes found I was quietly crying. He never looked at me the rest of that day. At the time I was upset by the pain and the humiliation. There was no rule against clouting children not your own and I didn't dare complain to my mother as I assumed she would simply say I deserved it for breaking the bowl. Years later I realised the spanking was a sexual thing for old Mayes because I could tell that from then on he looked for any excuse to do it again.

But then I couldn't understand why he was quite friendly when I worked one day a week and was now so permanently grumpy when I worked for him six days a week. I tried really hard and the bowl was pretty much the only thing I'd broken in all the time I'd worked for him. But children are vulnerable to adults because they always assume the adult is right whatever he or she does.

The bottom smacking happened a few more times and I just put up with it though it hurt and I always felt humiliated. He also used to leave his hand there after a few smacks or he'd pull up the side of my knickers so that the smacks were actually on my bare behind or on my leg which made it even more painful for me.

Then came a much worse turn of events. I was at home one Sunday and my mother smiled at me and said, 'Mr Mayes wants you to live in and he's going to increase your wages.'

I must have looked really upset because she came over and asked me what was wrong. I just couldn't tell her for some reason and she seemed so pleased that I found it impossible to make a fuss. I'd spent my life till then doing exactly what I was told. It was what children did then and all the smacking I'd received just made me feel that I was failing somehow. If I was being smacked it must be because I wasn't doing it right and I was most confused and upset, what with having no one to mention it to. I just cried at night – many nights – and told my mother in the morning that I had something in my eye to explain the blotchiness.

I was proud of the fact that I was really obedient and didn't want my mother to think that I was useless and constantly being punished. Being obedient was really prized back then. No one saw anything charming in a naughty child so I wasn't one. But I really didn't like Mr Mayes by now and dreaded making the slightest mistake that would give him the chance to spank me because I sensed that he was enjoying himself and looking out for every chance to do it again. And now of course there would be no escape in the evenings and at night as I would be sleeping in his house.

Chapter Eighteen

That first day when I carried my bag into old Mayes' house and knew I had to stay was probably the lowest point of my life. I worked for madder people than Mr Mayes later on but I was more experienced by then and could look after myself and make my own decisions. Back then I was only a teenager barely out of childhood and hadn't a clue about the world and old Mayes took advantage of that fact.

I noticed he went back to his friendly way of carrying on the day I arrived to stay full time. He was as he had been when I'd first worked for him on Saturdays. He showed me up to my room where he'd put a small jug of flowers – just the jug that I used when I did the same thing with flowers downstairs. The jug I thought he'd never noticed. But I didn't see it as a nice gesture because I was so scared of what was going to happen.

He left me in my room and I got changed into a dress my mother had made for me out of some blue cotton material. I didn't have to wear a cap, which was something you had to wear as a kitchen maid in a big house, but Mother said I should have a blue dress and apron and look the part a bit even if it was only for Mr Mayes.

I often wondered later on if she knew anything about

him at all before she allowed me to live there. But there was no way to check on him and there were so many odd people round about that no one would have thought his rabbit scarf and his bachelor ways were anything to worry about.

Although the spanking certainly had a sexual element about it at the time it never occurred to me for a minute because I'd never ever heard of sex. If you'd told me the mechanics of sex I'd have thought you were insane. I think I thought babies came from big expensive shops and if someone had told me that babies came from *there* after *that* I think I'd have fainted.

Unfortunately, money was always so tight in those days that in trying to keep body and soul together parents often didn't see what was right in front of their noses. They'd send their children off to all sorts of dangerous work with people who really shouldn't have been trusted at all. No one could admit to children that sex existed at all, let alone that some people liked the idea of having sex or doing sexual things to children. When Mr Mayes paid my father and mother a bit more for me to stay with him they thought it was just because he wanted his house kept clean and his meals cooked for him. I think they also had some wild idea that when I was sixteen he might marry me and I'd get his house, you see. It would not have occurred to them that he might do weird things to me in the meantime or that there might be something wrong with a sixteen-year-old marrying a man of fifty!

For now I had to cope with the fact that I had to sleep in an attic that was really scary because there were holes in the ceiling and I heard bats and mice fluttering and scuttling about when I was trying to sleep. Mayes also kept his dead mother's clothes in a great heap in the attic room next to mine along with half a dozen stuffed fish. I think he'd stuffed them himself because there was a constant disgusting smell of preserving chemicals. But if the downstairs rooms were dark and gloomy the stairs and upper rooms hadn't seen the light for centuries. Through a gap in one old wooden panel I could see the twigs and mud that made up the wall between the timbers. What a primitive world that was!

Now that I was with Mr Mayes the whole time he decided to get as much work as possible out of me. And whenever he asked me to do something he leaned towards me with that old leer of his. I think it was his idea of a charming smile!

When I'd been there on Saturdays, and later working as a day maid, it had been fairly relaxed. But that all changed now. As soon as I finished one task he was at me to start another and if he couldn't think of anything else he made me chop firewood, which was almost impossible for a young girl. I managed by cutting kindling from the smaller logs rather than attempt the bigger ones. Those I could hardly move, but it was back-breaking work and he normally kept me at it from seven in the morning till eight at night.

On one occasion when he didn't like something I'd done he made me stand outside in the rain for half an hour. He also kept a small square of paper in the corner of the kitchen and at other times if he wasn't happy with something he would make me stand on it for half an hour. If I moved off the paper before he told me to he would spank me. Why the hell I didn't just tell him to get lost or throw something at his head I don't know. Youth and inexperience I suppose.

Years later when I told my mother what he'd done she was really upset and asked me why I hadn't told her what was going on. I told her that she'd seemed so keen on my having the job that I couldn't bear to disappoint her and that at the time I'd thought the spankings were because I wasn't doing a good job. And there was no doubt at the time that she and my father were delighted with the money Mr Mayes paid. I could see the relief in their eyes when they asked me each Sunday how I was getting on. I could see they were desperate that I should be happy with the job too so I didn't ask about leaving. I don't blame them. That's just the way it was then.

But I'm still amazed when I look back that I put up with it so long. I was there for more than a year before I finally realised I'd had enough.

Chapter Nineteen

The final straw came when I was in bed one night asleep and some time in the early hours I woke and realised that Old Mayes was sitting on the end of my bed. I stayed as still as I could, hardly breathing and, despite all that had happened, still amazed that he could find yet another way to frighten me.

Time stopped. I didn't move and he didn't move. It sounds odd but I remember being both scared and calm at the same.

Then, after perhaps five minutes, he stood up and wandered over to the little window, walked up and down a few times and then climbed into bed with me.

Without a word he rolled on top of me and all I can recall now is the horrible smell – sweat and smoke and dead rabbit. He weighed a ton too and I felt I was stuck under a mountain. I was so astonished it didn't seem as if it was happening to me. Then he began to run his hands all up and down my front and he tried to force my legs apart. It was horrible.

I didn't scream but I started to cry and wail, though stupidly I only wailed in a half-hearted way as if there were other people around and I should try not to disturb them. He was scuffling at me and breathing loudly and then I became a little hysterical because I couldn't breathe. I started thrashing around and kicking. I think this must have scared him a little as he lifted his weight as if to look down at me and I was able to slip out from under him.

I went downstairs where I slept on the sofa and cried for the rest of the night.

In the morning I went slowly up to my room listening all the while and ready to run away if I heard him. He had gone. In a strange way I felt bad about what had happened as if I had done something wrong, but whatever else I knew, I knew I couldn't stay.

I packed my bag, put my coat on and walked down the stairs thinking I probably wouldn't see him on the way out. I didn't want to see him but I wasn't really afraid at all. I knew now that none of what had been happening was right. I didn't quite know why it was wrong but I remember feeling it was a bit like having a bad dream or reading a scary book. But it was also really embarrassing. How could I talk to someone about chickens and onions when the night before they'd heaved their smelly carcase on top of me and dribbled on my face?

Anyway it was a good job I was feeling determined because he appeared as I reached the bottom of the stairs and he smiled. He then reached across to hand me a grubby bit of paper that would have had the day's duties written on it.

I've never forgotten what I did next. I was so proud of myself. I looked him in the eye, screwed up the paper and threw it as hard as I could in his face. I don't know what he did after that because I never looked back. I turned and walked straight out the door and never saw him again.

As I marched up the narrow lane away from his house for ever I realised I was going to have to come up with some kind of an explanation for my mother, but I was lucky because she'd been thinking I should start a proper job in a bigger house anyway.

Mayes paid her quite well for my work but not nearly as much as I would get in Norwich or in a big country house. So when I got back and told her I hated Mayes and wasn't going back she never said a word. Mind you, she didn't really ask me what had happened either. People didn't tend to go into things so much in those days. They'd say, 'There's trouble . . .' and then exchange knowing looks as if to say we all knew there would be but we don't want to dirty our mouths by discussing it. I suppose we were all a bit emotionally repressed by modern standards. You just put up with things and in my mum's case she couldn't bear trouble or arguments and she knew she'd bump into Mayes now and then so it was better she didn't know the details or there might be a huge row. Also I wouldn't have known what to say. Him getting into bed with me seemed just disgusting but I couldn't have said anything about it from a sexual point of view because talking about it in those days was worse than doing it!

Mum never mentioned all this hullabaloo to my dad either. She let him think that it was all part of her plan to get me a better job in town or at least in a bigger house.

With one exception, I never had much luck with men and I've often wondered if it might have been because of what happened with Mr Mayes. He was certainly a horrible introduction to what men could be like. Not that

I'm saying all men are like him, but how I wished I'd had the presence of mind to put a bucket of slops over his head. And of course I wish I'd had a longer childhood so I could have been a teenage girl with a teenage boyfriend. That seems impossibly romantic to me, but they hadn't invented teenagers when I was young!

Ten years later I heard that old Mr Mayes died while walking the fields and as it was summer he'd almost rotted away by the time he was found. They identified him by his wallet and clothes mostly. That was quite common in rural areas – I mean to die somewhere remote and not be found for a while. A farmer would go out and have a heart attack in a field and if he had no family he might not be missed for days or weeks. We didn't have telephones you see and we didn't write letters to each other either, so people could disappear.

Chapter Twenty

I stayed at home for a few weeks after leaving Mr Mayes. In fact I hardly left the cottage and I think if it had been in more recent times you'd have said I was depressed or having a bit of a breakdown, but youngsters are resilient, or at least I was.

When my mother said she'd found me a job as a kitchen maid in a big house about ten miles away I was delighted and not just because it was ten miles from that old devil Mayes.

My father borrowed a pony and an old trap to take me to my new job, but neither he nor my mother explained who the people were I'd be working for. All I knew was that they were farmers in a much bigger way than Mr Mayes and, as I was to discover, they had ideas that they were quite grand.

Rumbling along in that old trap we would have looked like something from the nineteenth century, I'm sure. It was woodwormed and rickety and the paint had mostly flaked off so it was nothing like the carts you see on television – all bright in the sun and with a prancing pony at the front. Our old cart was pulled by a very downtrodden pony and I wasn't much better myself. I was such a dowdy thing with shabby clothes sponged down a bit to make them look presentable and the style of my father's suit was at least fifty years out of date. My father wore flat-fronted trousers. Trousers with creases were worn by the better-off but they'd have been too much extra work for a working man. And there was no such thing as working clothes then – you just had clothes you wore all the time and maybe, if you were lucky, a suit for Sundays.

The lanes were quiet and we were sitting high up and I remember enjoying the journey. We even saw a car or two which was exciting for me.

The house where I was to work was one of those red-brick farmhouses like a great big box with its front door in the centre and three stories high. It was built I think in the 1780s or 1790s or at least that's what one of the staff told me later. To me, on that day, it was enormous compared to Mr Mayes' farmhouse and you could have fitted our cottage in the outhouse.

For reasons I've never understood we got down from the trap and walked the last part of the way up the drive and to the door at the back of the house. We could have driven round but my father wouldn't do it. I think it was a deference thing – my father didn't want to seem to presume to drive up the gravel to the house in case it looked arrogant or as if he thought he was something more than a servant.

There we are you see, that status thing again. He was afraid of seeming proud of himself and what he was.

The door at the back was down a short flight of steps and under a small metal awning. I remember noticing how tiny it was compared to the very grand door at the front.

We knocked and a large middle-aged woman with a beautiful pure white apron came to the door and ushered me in. My father whispered to me, 'Be good, Nancy,' but was too shy to kiss me as he left.

I was a little more used to the rough edge of life by now and wasn't much afraid when he disappeared even though I knew I wouldn't see him for months. I also knew I couldn't stay at home for ever. I had to get on.

Mrs Spencer, the woman in the white apron, was the cook. She seemed nice enough and almost the first thing she told me was that I was to have a half-day off each week on a Wednesday. I found out later that it was standard practice for servants to get a half-day off each week *and* every other Sunday but Mrs Spencer never mentioned the Sundays and I was such an innocent I just nodded and accepted what she said. You could have told me pretty much anything then and I would have accepted it. It was only later I realised how ridiculous it was never to question anything. 'Half a day a week is more than enough for a young girl,' said Mrs Spencer. 'It's just time to get into trouble. There's nothing to do round here except cause mischief wandering about anyway and you will have a great deal of very interesting work here.'

But Mrs Spencer was a kind woman under a slightly cold exterior. She sat me down in the kitchen and quizzed me to find out how much I knew about working in a big kitchen. I told her about cooking for Mr Mayes and I could see she wasn't much impressed. She was quite right too because he hadn't taught me a thing, not properly anyway. I tried to make it sound as if I'd cooked lots of different things for him but of course I hadn't – just rabbit stew and pigeon and chicken broth of one kind or another.

She asked me about all sorts of strange-sounding dishes I'd never heard of. When I shook my head each time she must have put me down for a very poor sort of girl, which of course I was.

She was very proud of the fact that she could cook French dishes. Among the wealthy at that time French cooking was all the rage – they liked quenelles and consommés and that sort of thing. Not really adventurous but anything French had a sort of aura about it, so cooks up and down the country learned what they could and a bit of that fancy stuff even drifted into the Norfolk countryside.

The grandest houses would employ men to do the cooking – chefs who really were brought over from France. They would look down at someone who had a cook who wasn't French but knew a few French dishes, and that sort of cook – like Mrs Spencer – would in their turn look down on anyone who could only cook steak and kidney pudding and Irish stew and knew nothing at all about France. It was as my father used to say, tuppence ha'penny looking down on tuppence.

But at least I knew how to chop vegetables and dig them up and I knew what the different kinds were, although I was to learn about a few odd buggers in this kitchen that I'd never come across before – including artichokes and asparagus, neither of which I ever really saw the point of.

That first morning Mrs Spencer said to me, 'Well, we might as well start at the beginning.' She then took me over to the wall where I'd already noticed there were some sheets of paper pasted up. Each paper had a list of recipes: an entrée, a soup, meat course, fish course, pudding and sometimes another savory. They were the house menus and Mrs Spencer explained that the couple we worked for never changed the recipes and never changed the order in which they came round each week.

That probably sounds odd but it didn't seem so strange to me as I'd grown up in a house where we ate the same few dishes all the time. It was always potatoes and cabbage or potatoes and carrots or potatoes and turnip occasionally livened up by a bit of pork or a pigeon.

We were on the Friday menu, explained Mrs Spencer, as this was a Friday. But she also pointed out that the family sometimes had the Friday menu on other days if they fancied a change and the Wednesday menu might be requested on a Saturday. Completely mad, I thought, but then everything in my life till now – and later on for that matter – seemed mad to me in lots of ways. But then life's a rum go, isn't it? We're all a bit mad, aren't we?

So we were on the Friday menu. Mrs Spencer put out salt and pepper, cans of stuff, bottles, a few pots of spices and bags of leaves I couldn't identify and finally she carefully laid out a number of knives and sieves, pots and pans. Each had its own space and they were arranged in a precise pattern. Then she said, 'Nancy, that's the Friday stuff. I want you to remember where I've put it and what it is and I want you to put it in your book.'

'I don't have a book.' I said

'You don't have a book? What have you been taught?' she said in a cross voice.

She straight away marched out of the kitchen tut-tutting at the top of her voice and came back five minutes later with a tall, narrow-lined ledger book. She gave it to me.

'You won't remember a thing without this. Write

down everything I tell you in it, especially the way I cook things. The method I mean. I might not be the world's greatest cook but if you write everything down you can take the book from job to job and you'll know all the recipes. The cook's bible is her own private recipe book. Always remember that.'

And do you know that was the best piece of advice I was given in all my years as a domestic. I kept my book until I finally retired and though it was horribly dog-eared by then and I knew most of the contents off by heart, I treasured it. As long as I had it I felt safe because, by the end, it had everything in it from recipes for simple English dishes to complicated French nonsense – it even had a few curries and Italian dishes in it.

I'd hardly taken my coat off on that first day before I was trying to do everything Mrs Spencer told me to do. Cook had a room downstairs that was called the stew-ard's room, even though she lived in it and she definitely wasn't the steward. I went in Mrs Spencer's room a few times and thought this was the sort of room I would like. It seemed so luxurious to me. It had a rug, a small fire – that I was supposed to light every morning – a table and chair, a sofa and even a small bookcase and a window looking out over the garden. And once again I thought, 'Oh, I so want to be a cook and have all these nice things!'

After we'd laid out the table ready for the cooking itself to start, she took me up the servants' staircase.

Chapter Twenty-One

My room was at the top of the house, where the servants – well, except perhaps the senior servants – usually lived in a big house. It meant that the family didn't have to climb so many stairs to get to their beds. We country girls on the other hand were thought to be tough types capable of walking twenty miles or up a hundred flights of stairs.

As the attic rooms were meant for junior servants they had low ceilings, cheap thin doors, no fireplaces and not a scrap of anything warm or decorative. As we walked up, Cook told me that my room had originally been divided into a row of tiny rooms for about eight servants – and even coming from my little cottage that sounded impossible to me! But it must have been true because you could see where the thin plaster partitions had once been.

My little garret room had a very low ceiling – certainly less than six feet high – and it ran about half the length of the house. It was about seven feet wide and twenty feet long so a very strange shape and blow me over, how the wind came in through the three little dormer windows! I could have flown a kite in that room!

If you stood on a chair there was a view across the

countryside, but I think I could have done without the view to save a bit of body heat because the window frames were rotten and you could see daylight through a two-inch gap all along the bottom of one window. Imagine that in winter with me curled up under three thin blankets and an inch of ice on the glass. There was, as I say, no fireplace at all, so no heating. But I must admit that I would have been far more surprised if there *had* been heating since we had none at home and I'd never heard of anyone having heating in a bedroom before. The windows were about two feet square and they couldn't be seen from the ground outside the house because there was a parapet in front of them.

During the time I slept at that house – more than two years in all I think – I was often convinced I saw an apparition on that parapet. We were too far from any trees for the shadow I saw flitting by at night to be the shadow of a branch and it seemed to me there was nothing else that could have made that strange dark rush across the small windows and ceiling. It would go past once and then appear a second and then a third time before finally disappearing. And I always saw it if I woke, as I often did, in the early hours when it was still very dark. I was really scared but when I finally mentioned it to Mrs Spencer she said, 'Don't be silly – it's the flag on the pole.'

Now there *was* a flag on a pole high above the house but I could never convince myself it caused that rushing shadow, because the shadow always ran the whole length of the twenty-foot-long room before disappearing. How could the shadow of a flag do that? I'm sure there is no connection, but years later I told the story of the shadow on the parapet, as I used to call it, to another servant and she told me she knew the house I was talking about and that she'd heard that a young servant at the end of the nineteenth century had gone mad in the house and one day, when she wasn't being watched, had got up from her bed and run along the parapet before falling to her death.

Perhaps it was the flag on the pole, but I'm glad I didn't know the story of the servant while I lived in that room.

Mind you I was so tired each night when I went to bed that it perhaps wouldn't have bothered me anyway. I used to wake up for a minute, see the rushing shadow, wonder if I should be more scared and then fall asleep as if I'd been hit on the head.

Chapter Twenty-Two

Mrs Spencer worked very hard herself and seemed to have no life at all away from the house nor any desire for one and this, I think, was why she expected me to work almost continually. She just couldn't understand why anyone would want any time off at all.

When my first Wednesday came round I was so longing for a little time away from bloody onions and beef and gravy and the rest of it. I'd been hard at it from six in the morning until about twelve-thirty, lunchtime. I knew I had only half an hour left before I would be free for the afternoon and evening. I was counting the minutes on the big kitchen clock high up on the wall over the range. Mrs Spencer had hardly spoken that morning but she suddenly told me that the housemaid was sick and all the bedrooms and other family rooms needed cleaning. 'Don't worry that you've never done it before,' she said. 'I'll give you a little list of things to do and no one will mind if it's not quite as it would normally be. They know you're a beginner and won't expect too much.' She smiled as she said this, as if she was doing me a favour.

I replied, 'But it's my afternoon off. I've been looking forward to it.'

I was so shocked that I began to cry right in front of her. Terrible really. And then she said, more kindly, 'Now don't be silly. You'll just wander around and waste the time or get into trouble. And what could you do anyway except walk the roads. So get on with you now. You'll get to see the rest of the house and won't that be fun?'

It was the matter of fact way she dismissed my need for time off that really upset me. Whenever I thought of that moment in later years the stab of pain would come back. It was such a disappointment because without a little time off now and then you might as well have been in prison. I was already developing a bit of a thick skin after my experience with Mr Mayes but this was too much to bear and I was so tired. But disappointments were our lot in life so I had to get on with it.

That afternoon, when I should have been out enjoying at least some fresh air, I gradually worked my way round first the bedrooms and then the sitting rooms. They seemed very smart and very grand to me but somehow gloomy too. Half the things that lay about on tables and chairs I had never seen before.

In one room the walls were covered from about four feet above the floor right up to the ceiling with dozens of dreary pictures in heavy frames. Not a space of wall was visible behind them. In another room a human skeleton hung from a hook on the wall which made me thank my lucky stars that I didn't have to clean regularly. I mentioned the skeleton to Mrs Spencer and she laughed and said that it was there because the boss was a doctor, but I still think it was a horrible thing to have in the house. Mrs Spencer told me it was the skeleton of a man who had been hanged in Norwich in the 1850s. She said that if I looked closely at the wall behind the skeleton I would see a small label with the name of the man and the date he was executed. Needless to say I never took a peek.

In one of the bedrooms I found something very shocking. The sheets in the master's bedroom, which I'd been told to roll up and bring down for washing, were covered in blood and what looked like faeces. It was horrible but when I mentioned it to Mrs Spencer – I was always reporting back to Mrs Spencer! – fearing I might in some way be blamed for the state they were in, she simply said, 'Our job is just to work for them, not ask what they get up to.' But later on when I got friendly with the housemaid she told me the sheets were often like that. She said the doctor got up to all sorts when his wife was away, and she often went away to visit her family in London.

I thought this was probably just talk but on a few occasions late at night over the coming months and especially at the weekends I heard the sounds of loud partying going on half the night and then on the Monday they'd all be gone and the house would be quiet, waiting for the return of its mistress.

I saw the doctor a few times and he looked so respectable coming back from his work. But I also saw him a few times coming back to the house at night when his wife was away with two, sometimes three, women and they'd be drunk, laughing and singing or shouting. You'd hear them all night.

People think that everyone behaved in a more moral fashion in the past but it's nonsense – they were just a lot sneakier back then. That doctor was always up to no good. I remember once going upstairs to collect something and I heard screams and all sorts of grunts coming from his bedroom — again when his wife was away. The noise was like a series of animal squeals and groans and the floorboards and wall were thumping away like mad. I was never a prude despite the fact that I never married but I wondered that time why on earth they couldn't have been a bit quieter. You could hear them even in the kitchen and during the afternoon.

When Mrs Spencer was in one of her chatty moods she said to me, 'You always know when he's having his wicked way because the dogs start howling.' And do you know, she was right because a few times after that I noticed that when he went into town and came back with a couple of girls he'd go upstairs with them, and sure enough shortly afterwards the two dogs would start a terrific clatter. When I got used to the goings-on it used to make me laugh but like a good domestic I didn't care a bit about his morals — I was more worried about the state of the sheets.

I sometimes wondered if all this slightly sordid sex didn't put me off a bit. It's true I was no delicate princess but a big strong country girl — that was the phrase used about girls with my sort of figure. I was no longer skinny. I'd developed in all sorts of directions and looked as if I could carry a chest of drawers on my own!

After my stint as a housemaid on that one afternoon and evening I was confirmed for ever in my view that the kitchen was much the best, and safest, place to be despite the fact that it frequently involved the most awful jobs.

Chapter Twenty-Three

Eels. A boy used to deliver them now and then and still alive. The doctor used to make up some preparation or other using them, but just think of them coming to the kitchen alive. The poor things can live quite a time out of water so we'd get them still slithering in bundles of wet grass in a sack. They were caught by an old Fen man whose family had been eel catchers for generations – or so Mrs Spencer said. Certainly the boy who delivered them was a rum one. He was always filthy. A blackened face like a sweep and his clothes as greasy and stained as you can imagine. That's something you don't see today. When people's clothes get really dirty they don't just look grubby, they get a sort of slimy sheen. It was common to see it back then because there were no baths for the poor and they got by with a bit of a face wash now and then and pretty much nothing else. And if they didn't wash their bodies they certainly didn't wash their clothes.

So there we were with a sack of slippery eels. Mrs Spencer hated this part of her job so she'd fortify herself with a cup of tea and then tip them out into the biggest of the kitchen's three zinc-lined sinks. There might be half a dozen or more and they'd be a bit slow by now, having been out of water so long, but they never stopped moving and I could see their green eyes moving too.

I watched her killing them and vowed I'd leave any job where they asked me to do it. She put a leather glove on one hand and got a big chopping board ready next to the sink. With her jaw and lips set firm and a terrible grim look in her eyes she leaned in and grabbed the first one, lifted it on to the board and quickly cut its head off. The others would follow one after another. It was like a bloody execution. Horrible. The eels with their heads gone would still be thrashing around in the sink.

Mrs Spencer would stop and have another cup of tea and wait till the writhing stopped. She'd then nail each dead eel to an upright beam in the wall just outside the back door. Once the eel was firmly fixed she would pull the skin off it using the same thick glove rubbed with salt to get a grip through the slime.

We had all sorts of horrible tasks like this to do now and then. I had some even worse ones in houses where I worked later on. And despite my vow never to do any eel killing I had no choice in the end and had to do it.

Chapter Twenty-Four

Mrs Spencer was a loyal sort of old-fashioned servant, but her loyalty got her nowhere because, about a year after I arrived, they got rid of her. She was really upset and I found her crying in the kitchen. I was amazed that this big strong woman should be reduced to this and that the doctor and his wife would let her go at the drop of a hat after all the years she'd worked for them.

'Ten years,' she said tearfully as I stood awkwardly near her chair.

'Ten years and now this.'

She had worked selflessly for them with hardly even an afternoon off. She had never had a holiday and only occasionally would have an hour or two to herself. I wanted to say to her, 'That's why you should take your afternoons and Sundays off. They won't be any nicer to you if you don't.'

I really think she thought they would keep her for ever because she was so hard-working and uncomplaining and never asked for a pay rise.

But there we are. It was a lesson I learned and learned well.

Loyalty only counted one way in domestic service. You were to be grateful and loyal; but they could drop you in a second when it suited them. Oh, it made my blood boil and I instantly forgot all about the fact that Mrs Spencer and I had had our little tiffs. They had told her they could no longer afford her wages and in those days that was enough. No redundancy money, no apology and no care for what she might do now. When you lost your job as a domestic you lost your home as well. It made me determined not to end up in the same position.

There was a hidden pattern in this. Mean-hearted employers would get a cook and eventually encourage her to train one of the senior kitchen maids – or the only kitchen maid if there was just one – and then when they felt the maid knew enough (and had filled in the recipes in her book) they'd make an excuse and get rid of the cook, who was more expensive. The maid would then cook and do a bit of housework. That's what happened here.

Mrs Spencer got another job quickly enough and even though I think she knew that the doctor and his wife had treated her very badly she still insisted I copy a few more recipes into my book – her 'specials' as she described them – so they could continue to eat what they enjoyed. She also dictated notes to me on various recipes and tricks of the trade that I still referred to fifty years later. Old Spencer was a nice enough woman under a hard exterior but hard exteriors were more important then for the lower classes who got so buffeted by bad luck, miserable jobs, low pay and no one to look after them.

Chapter Twenty-Five

After Mrs Spencer left I was terrified I wouldn't be able to manage the kitchen as I'd only helped her until now and I'd hardly been working for a year, but my experience with Mrs Spencer and the doctor had already taught me how the world of domestic service really worked.

You see, when there were no laws to protect servants then inevitably the servants were asked to do more and more for less and less. If you didn't like it you had to leave because there was always another poor mug desperate for a job. What's really strange is that the doctor and his wife would certainly have thought of themselves as decent, fair-minded people but the truth is that they felt no obligation to be decent to the servants, only to their equals or superiors.

So having taken poor Mrs Spencer's job I got on with it as best I could. I followed the Saturday recipe for dinner on the first day after Mrs Spencer left.

Until that day Mrs Spencer had always cooked enough so that we could have our food too, so we had what the family had. By we, I mean the housemaid, the kitchen maid and the cook. Now of course it was just the two of us – me, the kitchen maid trying to pretend to be cook, and the housemaid.

That first evening, with a mass of vegetables and meat flying everywhere, the doctor's wife came in without the traditional knock. I say the traditional knock because it was a rule that the mistress of the house – even the grandest mistress in the grandest house – always knocked before she came into the cook's domain. It was the only bit of deference shown to those below stairs, but clearly I hadn't yet earned that privilege.

In she came in a great bustle of skirts. We looked at each other and there was a pause. Then she said: 'Now that you are cooking for us I want you to make sure you cook only enough for the family. Mrs Spencer was rather wasteful you know.'

I didn't quite know what she was getting at so she explained without a hint of embarrassment that from now on I was to cook two lots of food. Where Mrs Spencer had cooked enough for the family and the servants I was to cook two sets of dishes for each meal. The family would carry on having what they normally had but I was to buy only the cheapest stewing steak and rabbit for myself and the housemaid.

While I was employed as a kitchen maid the doctor's wife had hardly glanced at me on the few occasions we had been in the same room together and I'd hardly looked at her. But I did now. She was a strange-looking thing, much older than the doctor. She had her silver-streaked hair up in a bun in quite an old-fashioned style and she wore a narrow silk dress that came past her knees. This was the height of fashion at the time. She had a very grey complexion and I remember thinking how odd it was that a doctor should have such a sickly-looking wife. Given what I knew of the doctor's carryings-on I think his wife was probably depressed, which explained the tense grey face and an odd twitch of the mouth that I noticed every time she spoke to me

The doctor himself I hardly ever saw. He never came down to the kitchen and I would just occasionally glimpse him going out of the house or coming back. He was always very soberly dressed in a dark suit and he carried his doctor's bag all the time. The housemaid told me she'd been told never to touch or move or even dust his bag if she saw it. She also told me he took it out with him when he went on what she called his sprees. She meant his little night-time outings when his wife was in London.

Anyway, the doctor's wife never smiled and she certainly didn't smile now. She told me in a slightly irritated, almost cross tone – as if I'd already done something wrong – that from now on I was to bring all the cooked food, the family's and the servants', to the dining room, where the doctor would serve a plate of food for me that I was then to take back to the kitchen and eat there with the housemaid. She also said we were not to talk to each other during meals.

So from then on every day, like a couple of humble paupers, we filed into the dining room where the doctor dished the meat and vegetables on to two plates and then handed them to us without a word. It was so humiliating that I couldn't stop my face from burning red each time we had to do it – which, don't forget, was every day. And if he wasn't there, she would dish up the food. At night I used to cry because this seemed so unbearable and especially after I thought that I'd had a sort of promotion. Of course it was no promotion at all. By now I missed Mrs Spencer and what seemed like much better days.

Innocent and ignorant as I was and used to doing what I was told, I still thought this was a disgusting way for a well-educated person to behave, a person with money and position. Luckily after a few weeks the doctor and his wife began to get fed up with the rigmarole of serving our food and it was abandoned. No doubt they realised it meant more work for them as well as us. After six months he would insist on serving our food only now and then when he remembered or, presumably, when he was in a bad mood or in a panic about money.

Despite that slight reprieve I still had to cook separate cheaper meat every lunch and dinnertime for myself and the housemaid.

Even with my poor background I knew that this was all wrong. It made me angry but I also felt sorry for the doctor that, with his education, he could behave far worse than an illiterate farm worker.

The doctor was a bad sort altogether. He seemed to dislike everyone. The housemaid used to tell me that she overheard him saying to his wife that he would never treat blacks, gypsies or Irish people. Once there was a commotion and I peered out of the kitchen window. There I saw the doctor waving his arms and shouting at a small group of gypsies who had presumably come to ask for some medicine. He didn't even wait to see what was wrong or to find out if they could pay.

The gypsies looked dignified and resigned and without a word they trailed off back down the drive. I thought of how those gypsies had treated me as a child. I thought, they may be poor travellers but they are better people than you with all your money and your fine pills and potions.

So I didn't have much respect for the doctor. Like a lot of so-called professionals back then he thought he was better than everyone else. I'm sure there were lots of good doctors then but doctors had a bad reputation I can tell you, particularly among poor people. The trouble was that when someone was really ill most doctors wouldn't treat them – even if they were at death's door – unless they'd been paid first. When I was on door-opening duties I used to see all sorts of desperate people come and, unable to pay the doctor, they would offer all sorts of things to him. One man came with a bag of rabbits as payment; someone else came with an old silk hat. Another offered to work in the doctor's garden for a week if he would see his wife. But I had strict instructions from the doctor that he would only see those who could pay cash and the 'better sort', as he used to put it.

I think he was a terrific snob and what a hypocrite he was with all those visits from the women of the town, as we used to call them. I wish I'd had the courage to tell his wife! I felt so bad when I turned the desperate away. I gave the man with the rabbits a shilling from my own money and the man who offered to do the garden also got a shilling, which I could ill afford but it was a pitiful situation.

I stayed in that job much longer than maids usually stayed in a first real job, partly of course because of my fake promotion. Most maids were brave about going for promotions and new jobs regularly because it meant more money, and by the 1920s the old idea that you should stay in a job for life was disappearing. But in rural areas where you were quite isolated we tended to move a little less often, at least at first. Employers liked country girls for that very reason – they wouldn't move as frequently and they were thought to be harder working and more docile than town girls. In other words they wanted servants who would knuckle under and put up with anything without a word of complaint. But when I was about eighteen or nearly nineteen I started to look around.

I'd put up with being given scraps like a dog for a year and more by then because they never employed another proper cook or a kitchen maid to help me and I really thought my cooking had come along well enough to keep the miserable so-and-sos happy. Otherwise I would certainly have been sacked.

Chapter Twenty-Six

It was at the village fete that year that I realised what I was missing. I got talking to a girl from a big house about two miles away. She worked for an MP and local landowner and the house had ten full-time servants, she told me. When I told her about my duties she was astonished at how much I had to do single-handed.

'You want to get out of there,' she said. 'You can't carry on like that, and why should you. You mean you never have your time off? Should be bloody illegal.'

Apart from a few lonely wanders round the village in my early days and one or two visits home to my mum and dad I'd worked seven days a week from six in the morning till late at night for two years and more.

My new friend was amazed and I felt such a fool suddenly for putting up with it for so long. She told me that she had every Wednesday afternoon from twelve o'clock off and that if the family tried to keep her back – which they never did – she would leave and they knew it so she always set off prompt. She also got every other Sunday off. I'd never had a regular Sunday off. I didn't know it was standard practice and I've always wondered how many girls like me were just left year after year to work full-time ten or twelve hours a day and seven days a week. If people can exploit you they will – that's why the law should protect people, but especially young girls.

After that day at the fete I began to think about it and on my next day home about three months later – I still hadn't had the courage to tell the doctor I should have every other Sunday off – I told Mum I was thinking of leaving.

'Good idea,' she said. 'Have a look at the newspapers.'

I told her about the lack of time off, the low pay and the humiliating business with meals and I could see she was angry. Lots of mothers in those days encouraged their children to keep any terrible old job at all costs but that's what I loved about my mum; she wasn't afraid of change even in the Norfolk wilds.

Poor Mum was a tiny thing, completely unlike me in build, with blue eyes and light brown hair that kept its colour till she died a few years later. She'd been blonde as a girl. Dad was much bigger and stronger and I took after him, at least physically. He had a broad face and dark hair just like me.

Still, when I returned to the doctor's house after my mother reassured me about changing jobs it still took me six months to pluck up the courage to ask for what I should have had all along.

I went up and knocked on the door of the doctor's wife's sitting room, where I knew she would be at around eleven o'clock in the morning. She said 'Come in' in a friendly enough tone but immediately looked very unhappy to see it was me.

'Can I help you?' she said. Now she wasn't being snooty, I'll give her that, but she was very cold, very severe-looking. I used to wonder if she ever smiled about anything.

I said I was sorry to disturb her but that I must in future have a day off each week. I was so nervous that I muddled it a bit. I'd meant to say half a day each week and every other Sunday but I thought a day a week would do. My heart was racing as I spoke and it was awful how wobbly my voice sounded. It was so hard to keep my voice from going all over the place that I sort of blurted it out really.

I said I would like to have my first day off the follow-ing Wednesday and without waiting for a reply, I nodded, curtseyed, said thank you and left the room.

She never said a word and didn't mention it the next day when she came down for her usual early-morning visit to the kitchen to talk about the recipes for the day. But I noticed that she knocked before she came in and she looked less than her usual arrogant self. It was a revelation to me – I realised she felt she had lost control of something that had been important to her. Much later I thought she might have been a bit mad or driven slightly unbalanced by her husband's antics, because her visits to the kitchen were pointless. As I said earlier, the rota of meals each week didn't vary. In fact it only ever changed at the whim of the doctor, who I think was a bit of a bully.

So the following Wednesday I went home. I must admit I was such a silly that I left enough cooked food and cold dishes for the family to get them through the day, which meant that the night before I set off for home I had to work till one o'clock in the morning.

I'd asked the grocer's boy to ask the local carter to wait for me at the end of the drive but I can tell you, if he hadn't been there I'd have walked the ten miles home rather than spend my day off in that house.

It was a lovely morning and I enjoyed the journey. I remembered the first journey to the house in a similar cart and thought how much more I knew now than I knew then!

The carter didn't say much but I enjoyed the view across the fields, which were smaller back then before all the hedges were dug up to make it easier for the big machines. There's something very calming about travelling by slow coach. In fact this was one of the last times I went by horse-drawn transport as buses were coming in and spreading across the countryside. I'd like to say I missed the horse carts when they disappeared but it would be a lie. The buses didn't have to be organised and asked for like a cart or trap. They just came along and picked you up and they were much warmer in winter.

I walked the last bit to the cottage across a field and realised that this was the same route I'd gone to and from school all those years ago. Of course it wasn't that long ago really but it seemed an age to me.

Nothing had changed at home except the big strong parents I'd known as a child now seemed shrunken and weaker somehow. They were pleased to see me and my mother quickly told me she had an interview for a new job lined up for me. I hadn't had time to look in the papers – which were always a good way to find servant jobs – and I was impressed she had found something in what seemed no time at all. But the village grapevine was always good for servants' jobs. She told me it was in a house close to Norwich, as if its location was the most important thing. I think my mother thought that if it was close to Norwich with all its big city attractions it must be a good bet!

Anyway the upshot was that I could go for an interview whenever I was ready.

Chapter Twenty-Seven

When I went back to the doctor's house I felt really full of myself and was looking forward to telling them I planned to leave, but every morning when I tried to ask the doctor's wife if I could have a word with her she would rush off saying, 'Later, later, I'm far too busy.' Once she almost ran away and then she stopped coming down in the mornings. It was very odd. This went on for about a week and I was at my wits' end, especially as the more time that passed before I organised the interview the less the chance of my getting the new job.

I was so naïve – and my mother was too – that I thought the interview would lead to a definite job offer. I thought the interview was just the first part of the new job. I'd never been interviewed before. I'd just turned up and started work. It's very difficult for educated people to understand what it was like to know almost nothing. It's only when I look back from old age that I realise how little I knew – and not just about interviews!

But there's no doubt the doctor's wife had an inkling I wanted to leave. She was in a panic because they were getting so much out of me for so little. I'm sure they knew I was a complete innocent and that they were exploiting me, and they didn't want it to end in case they had to pay some older, wiser person the going rate.

In the end I ambushed her in the hall. I waited till mid-morning and stood just outside the servants' door from the hall to the stairs. As soon as I heard the sitting-room door open I leaped out and there she was.

Without giving her a second I said, 'I'm so sorry madam, but I wanted to tell you I will be leaving at the end of the week. I have a new situation.'

She looked furious and said I couldn't possibly have time off for an interview at their expense and that if I did attend an interview she would dock my pay by a whole week.

I felt myself go red in the face and had an almost overwhelming urge to cry but I was determined not to, because she was trying to bully me into staying. Young as I was I knew that much. I said no more and she looked daggers at me before disappearing back into the sitting room. I knew absolutely nothing about my rights or indeed if I even had any so far as docking my pay was concerned, but I just thought I would carry on with my work till the end of the week and see what happened.

But I had my revenge for all her horrible behaviour. Two weeks later there was another village fete, a really big one, and I think that in order to placate me a little the doctor's wife said I could spend a few hours at the fete. All the time I'd worked there, in the late evenings and at odd moments at the weekends when there was a lull in the work for an hour or two, I'd been doing little watercolour paintings. I'd never really stopped drawing and painting since that time my father had given me a few coloured chalks and some old grey paper when I was tiny. Before that I'd used bits of charcoal from the fire to scrawl things on odd scraps of paper and even once on the wall, for which I received a severe telling-off.

I even had a few watercolours in a little set that I'd bought myself and I was always painting scenes of fields and churches and cows. They were nothing much really as I only had a dozen colours and four brushes. But I heard there was to be an art competition at the fete in which anyone could enter a picture. On the day I went along with what I thought was one of my better efforts. It was only a landscape about ten inches by six inches but I was proud of it and asked the man on the art competition stand if I could be entered. He said my picture was very good and he'd be delighted to enter it.

I thought no more about it and wandered round on my own enjoying the fete. There were all the old-fashioned things you'd expect – jam and lemonade for sale, games for the children, a tug of war to be held between the boys from two villages. I had to curtsey to the doctor and his wife when I saw them but they just looked down their noses at me and walked on. But it didn't spoil my day because I was naturally optimistic like most young people and I loved the fete, which seemed special to me as I got out so rarely.

Chapter Twenty-Eight

Then as evening came on the local landowner presented the prizes to the children who had won the various races. There was also a prize for vegetables and one for the best flowers and then came the prize for the best picture.

I was hardly paying attention and sipping a little glass of lovely sweet home-made lemonade and looking around when I vaguely noticed a hush and people looking round. So, like a prize nitwit I started to look round, just copying everyone else. Then to my horror I heard the speaker saying, 'First prize for the best picture goes to Nancy Jackman. Is she here?' I put up my hand like a silly schoolgirl because I wasn't at all sure what to do next, but he beckoned me up to the front, smiled broadly at me and shook my hand. He wasn't angry or sneering or looking down at me. He said, 'Well done. A lovely picture. Well-deserved first prize.'

There was a round of applause and I can remember burning with embarrassment. Then I looked down and there was a whole pound note in my hand. I've never forgotten that moment and it would keep me scrawling for ever. I'd won something for the first time in my life! And no one was commenting on my poverty or my lack of education or on the fact that I was just a servant. I felt so good I was nearly bursting at the seams!

People say that at moments like that you float away on a cloud. Well it's true – I did.

But do you know what was best of all? I discovered later on that the doctor's wife had submitted a large watercolour in a gilded frame and she hadn't won a thing.

Chapter Twenty-Nine

When I got back to the house I found a note waiting for me asking me to leave at the end of the week. Clearly the doctor's wife's rage at being beaten in the art competition overcame her desire to keep me skivvying for her. I thought it was a bit rich dismissing me when I'd already said I was planning to leave.

The doctor came to give me my last wage and he did at least thank me for my work. After I left and went back to my parents' cottage I thought more about it and felt rather sorry for the doctor's wife. She had probably spent months on her picture and then paid to have it framed only to find she had been beaten by a servant, which would be very hard to bear. And of course painting may have been her escape from a horrible marriage just as it was my escape from a horrible job. On balance I thought I would rather have the horrible job than the horrible husband.

And of course the doctor's wife was as much a victim of the system as I was because the whole point of servants – or one of the important points about having them – was to give the well-off a sense of importance when they had no useful work to do. I'd taken away her sense of her importance, I think.

So I left and though my time with the doctor and Mrs Spencer had been hard, I had learned a lot. I had my little book of recipes and I could organise a kitchen and work as a cook with the best of them. Or so I thought. And the art prize had also given a huge boost to my confidence. I thought it was time I got a better job with time off and a proper cook's wages, but I was to be disappointed.

Back at the cottage my mother was her usual cheery self and delighted to have me home for a while. She told me the job she'd suggested for me before was still available and that I could go over any time to talk to the house-keeper about it.

So after a week spent helping my mother round the cottage I set off one morning for a big house just a few miles outside Norwich. I got a lift on a farm cart because although there were cars and buses by this time they were rare. I liked the idea of being closer to Norwich, which seemed to offer the excitement of the bright lights and busy streets after all my years in the quiet country-side. I thought, well, maybe this is just a stepping stone to real life.

The big house turned out to be just another old house – it certainly wasn't a palace – and my poor mother had got it all wrong. They wanted a maid-of-all-work not a cook because they already had a cook-cum-house-keeper. Months later when I mentioned this to my mother she looked baffled and said she'd been told there would definitely be some cooking and kitchen work so she'd assumed it was more or less a cook's position.

But I didn't mind. The cook-cum-housekeeper seemed a nice old thing – much nicer than Mrs Spencer

– when she met me at the door, but she had no more idea of an interview than I did. She thought I'd arrived to start work and it took a while for me to explain that I was just there to talk about a job.

She was a bit deaf, though.

'Oh it'll be fine,' she said. 'I will send the gardener with his cart to get your things tomorrow. Let me show you the kitchen now.' So that was that – I was back to being a maid!

The housekeeper-cook was Mrs Warren. She had a face that was amazingly battered and wrinkled but she moved about like a young thing. I had no idea how old she was. She told me that the man she worked for, who was a bachelor, lived on family money and had never had a job as far as she knew. She said he did nothing apart from write letters to the papers and occasionally travel to London and abroad. She then sat me down and said, 'I should tell you that he has a few odd habits.'

I had no idea what she might mean. But most of the men I'd known till now had some pretty odd habits, so I suppose I shouldn't have been surprised.

'He has a funny medical condition. It's nothing to be frightened of but he has little fits now and then and, sometimes, he comes into the kitchen and has them.'

'What sort of fits?' I asked. It sounded frightening.

'Well, he uses bad language and throws plates and crockery and other things around if he can get his hands on anything, which is why you'll always find I lock the cupboards if we're not at work. He might also shout at you but take no notice because he'll come down and apologise the next day. He always does.'

She was such a nice woman that I was reassured. Besides, I could hardly go all the way back home and tell my mother I didn't like the job. I'd be out of work then and always in my ears I could hear Mother saying, 'You have to work or you'll be in the workhouse.'

But my talk with Mrs Warren did make me think I'd gone from the frying pan into the fire. Looking back I realise that it wasn't so surprising. Lots of people who could employ servants and had enough money not to work became eccentric or mad as they got older. I'd say most domestic servants in those days would have told you the same thing. There were too many people who thought work of any kind was beneath them and as a result they did nothing; and doing nothing over very long periods makes a lot of people very odd. Only the very strong in my experience, or those who have a passionate hobby, can survive having nothing to do. I've always thought that doing nothing, no real work I mean, is much harder in some ways than having hard work to do.

I had a much nicer room in this house – the best I'd ever had in fact. I had a comfortable green armchair, a nice pine chest of drawers with five big drawers, a rug and even a big bookcase and, of all things, a mirror.

'Now my girl you can have a good look at yourself every day,' I said to myself, but I knew I wasn't much to look at. Homely I think was the word people used. I'd lost that young girl look that can make even the plain-est quite attractive for a while. But my problem was also that I put on weight easily and as I always tasted what I cooked it was never going to be easy. I'd always known I wasn't beautiful and though you'd think that might have made me sad, it didn't really because I had a sort of deeper confidence and happiness. I don't know where this came from, but even at school I knew it. Perhaps because my two best friends were both what they used to call strong, plain girls and we all know that children are always drawn to make friends with children who are physically similar to themselves. The three pretty girls in the class were always together. Mind you, I think later life was harder for them because they had airs and graces but they all had to do the same work we had to do in the end.

In my new job with my lovely room and nice old Mrs Warren to work for I thought I was in clover. I was a bit disappointed at being a general kitchen maid again, but I thought to myself, I know how to change jobs now and not rely on my mother to do it and get muddled. I thought, if I don't like this job in the end I'll be off to the big city in six months.

So far I had only one slight worry. Mrs Warren, lovely though she was, wouldn't tell me precisely why the last kitchen maid had left. She just changed the subject when I asked, but I had a feeling it had to do with the shouting and swearing she'd warned me about.

Chapter Thirty

On my first morning I was up with the lark and dressed and ready and really proud of myself because I thought, I'm really good at this now. I'm a professional. I went round the sitting rooms and morning room with my brushes, cleaned the stairs on my knees and was ready for a cup of tea by nine o'clock when I'd been told his lordship – he wasn't a lord at all but that's what we called him – would be having his breakfast.

I had my tea with Mrs Warren and was amazed at how she talked to me as if we were equals. That was very unusual, as I've said, because servants were as obsessed with status as their masters.

Having cleaned the rooms I helped make the breakfast and while we were at it I showed Mrs Warren my recipe book – the one I'd gradually added to in my previous job.

'Oh that's a very good idea but here we only have plain dishes,' she said. 'He eats about three different meals and hates it if they change even slightly. But you can add what we do here to your book because you never know what might happen.'

That was one of her favourite phrases. At least once a day she would say, 'Well we must do this or that because you never know what might happen.'

Like my father, Mrs Warren was a Methodist. Not straight-laced or puritanical but she was a type of domestic servant that was common then. She had always been single and always worked in other people's houses and never seemed to think she might have a life of her own. She went to church – or rather to the little chapel – nearby. She tried to encourage me to go and she was very respectable, but like her employer she had her eccentricities, as I found out later that first week

The breakfasts were always kidneys to start with – a big plate of them which I thought disgusting to get ready. This was followed by porridge made with milk, water and whisky. Now why he couldn't be like any other mortal and have the porridge *before* the kidneys I just don't know. I also had to take the sugar bowl up with the kidneys because he sprinkled sugar on everything he ate whether sweet or savoury.

That first day I got up the stairs as fast as I could, as the kidneys – about twenty of them – were still steaming. The master was sitting at the big table on his own but with two other places set. I curtseyed when I served him.

He didn't look up from his paper but just said, 'Always set for three, Daisy.' (Daisy was the previous maid's name.) 'Always three because you see you never know who might turn up.'

I thought he and Mrs Warren should have got married with their shared fondness for that little saying.

'Do you enjoy kidneys, Daisy?' he asked, still without looking up.

I couldn't be bothered to tell him that my name was Nancy so I just said, 'I don't know, sir, I've never tried them.'

'You should,' he said. 'It's the urine that gives them their flavour. I will ring if I need anything else.'

Not knowing what to think I had to ask Mrs Warren what he meant by urine when I got downstairs. I'd never heard the word before.

This was just the first in a series of odd incidents.

The rest of my first few days passed as such days usually pass below and above stairs. I cleaned the master's bedroom and then the other bedrooms though they looked as if they were never used.

Some girls always had trouble with their hands – they'd get chafed so badly that they'd bleed. They'd be red raw and never really toughen up. Well, mine got good and hard in no time at all. Like leather they were, but it made me worry because although I didn't think much about boys I just hoped I would one day get married and have a little boy of my own. That was the side of it I was interested in – the babies. But with my big strapping looks and hands like a stevedore I thought perhaps no boy would ever want me. I don't know how I thought I'd ever even meet a boy in the depths of the Norfolk countryside or stuck in the basement of an old house the whole time. I just sort of assumed it would happen as if by magic and without worrying about the details. How wrong I was!

Looking back I might have known it would be hard to meet someone I liked. I was a big red-faced girl – not fat but sturdy. Like most girls I wanted a nice handsome man who would adore me and treat me like a princess. I had ideas about a handsome man way above my station.

Anyway with my tough old hands I found the work in this new house not too hard and by the evening of that first day I was ready – little book in hand for any new tips I might learn – to help with the dinner.

Then came a bit of a surprise. Mrs Warren said we had the evening off as the master didn't want anything to eat and was out anyway.

'There's some cold meat in the pantry so help yourself to a bit of it,' she said. Then she put her coat on and disappeared out the door.

Well this was a right carry-on. I'd never been in this position before. I was all alone in the big house with nothing to do and assumed that I couldn't go out because one thing employers hated was to leave the house empty. In really big houses, aristocrats' houses I mean, they left a team of staff with little to do except the odd bit of dusting perhaps for months on end while they toured Europe or lived in another big house.

So I sat in the kitchen and ate some cold tongue. I was nervous about eating too much in case I was scolded later on. I ate it with a glass of water and some pickled walnuts. Everyone ate pickled bloomin' walnuts then. Don't ask me why. I think perhaps because they were a lively spicy taste and there was no Chinese or Indian food then! Most of what we ate by modern standards was really very plain, even dull.

After a while the spirit of curiosity got hold of me in a bad way. I was still young, you see, and a bit adventuresome. I wandered round the house and even sneaked a look in the master's rooms. I found one room that had high cupboards all around the walls. I opened the tall door of one of these cupboards and inside were narrow drawers stretching to the ceiling. I pulled one open and it was full of small scraps of torn paper. Thousands of them. I looked in the other drawers. They were all the same – filled with small scraps of torn paper.

In another room I found hundreds of children's toys,

boxes, play bricks, several rocking horses with the horse-hair stuffing coming out, big tin trains and cars, jigsaws chucked all over the place and a big clock, too. The clock must have been four feet high and four feet wide and you could see all the cogs and workings. It didn't look as if it had run for a hundred years as it was partly rusted and covered in dust. I never found out why that room was left like that. I was told not to clean it – ever, nor the room with the high cupboards filled with scraps of paper.

The next day Mrs Warren was back and we got on with our work. The days passed uneventfully and I got to know Mrs Warren quite well. I had to speak very loudly for her to hear me. She herself was softly spoken – or at least to me she was – and she told me she had grown up in Lincolnshire. She had been looked after by her grand-parents as a child after her father was killed by a kick from a horse. They had kept a shop that sold pets, feed-stuffs for farms, butter and eggs, groceries, clothing, newspapers, ink, seeds, timber, coal and medicine.

'It was such a lovely place to be as a child,' she often used to say.

'They'd have sold you anything,' she said, 'and if they didn't sell it they'd get it for you or make it for you. They'd have made you a coffin if you'd asked! It was always lively and busy in that shop and shopkeepers are a better class of person. They're looked up to by the community.

'Domestic service was a bit of a comedown for me, but you have to like it or lump it and accept whatever comes your way.'

Then she'd smile at me, pat my wrist and say, 'We'll get our reward. Don't worry.'

I think it was a phrase that comforted her and she got it from chapel of course and maybe there was something in it. I met many people who were comforted by the Bible. Mrs Warren certainly kept a copy and I found her reading it a few times. Once I saw her busily cooking and looking now and then at an open book and I thought, so she *does* use recipe books. But when I looked across I saw that she was actually consulting her Bible, which was covered in fat and grease marks and stains.

I say she was mild-mannered and quietly spoken but I heard the other side a few weeks later when the master had a small dinner party.

Chapter Thirty-One

I put my uniform on especially carefully that day and was told to make sure the rooms were extra thoroughly cleaned. Mrs Warren was I thought slightly anxious all day and somehow less friendly, but I paid no attention.

Two couples arrived at about eight in the evening and we had been told to get dinner ready for nine thirty. The noise of the people partying upstairs grew so loud that, as we cooked, we could hear it quite clearly deep in the basement.

Then when we were nearly ready with the soup I heard a clattering on the stairs and the master burst through the door shouting at the top of his voice with his tie all askew and his face almost purple.

I was shocked because he bellowed at Mrs Warren and at me and neither of us had done anything wrong.

I can't remember everything he said but this was roughly it: 'Where's my bloody dinner you useless bastard bitches? I want you out of here first thing in the morning. Out you go! Out. I'm not having this. Fuck off if you don't like it. Dirty rotten sluts. You're both bastards and you can fuck off.' And so on like a raving madman.

Mrs Warren's reaction was even more amazing.

'Would you like some hot chocolate?' she said in a calm voice.

'Get out, you bitch!' said the master.

'Come and sit here,' said Mrs Warren.

'No I fucking won't,' said he. But by now his seeming rage was subsiding and Mrs Warren, suddenly changing from her earlier calm, shouted back.

'Now come on, you get out of my kitchen. Get back to your guests you drunken fool. Go on. Off with you, off with you.'

And with that she pushed him out through the door and slammed it behind him.

I didn't ask her what this was all about. I didn't dare. But I was shaking when I took the soup up. I was sure I must be dreaming. This was madder than anything I'd ever seen before.

In the dining room, when I arrived with the soup tureen, the master sat with his guests as if nothing had happened. They didn't even look embarrassed though they must have heard him shouting and screaming down below in the kitchen.

I remember thinking, I'm going to have to get out of this house sooner rather than later!

Over the next few months I saw the master come down and shout and scream like this several times. He always did it when he'd had a few drinks or had visitors or – worst of all – both. And having witnessed it I can understand why the Temperance Society in those days tried to get people to take the pledge – I mean to stop drinking. In some people the effects were terrible.

On one occasion when the master was really drunk he came down and smashed about a dozen plates before Mrs Warren was able to bustle him out of the room. He threw them at the walls and the windows and one or two came frighteningly close to me. He then fell asleep in the hallway on the floor and, in the morning, I had to clear up a huge pool of vomit.

He never apologised to me when these things happened but Mrs Warren insisted that he always apologised to her. And certainly the day after he had a blow-up she would disappear upstairs for a bit. She used to say, 'Here we go. Off to see the penitent.' And her eyes would go up to heaven before she set off up the stairs for a private chat.

'He's harmless underneath it all,' she said. 'He just can't behave when he's had a drink.'

He was a funny-looking man. To go out he usually wore a frock coat and top hat with a fob watch and beautifully polished shoes which, unusually, he polished himself. I used to catch a glimpse of him through the window when I heard the door slam as he left. Sometimes he would dress like a tramp in shapeless baggy trousers, a filthy silk cravat and battered hat.

He probably was harmless but I'd really had enough of lunatics by now, so despite having only been in the job a few months I thought I'd keep an eye out for anything else that might be going. Rather than ask my mother to look for another job for me I thought I would do it myself – that way I could be sure I got the job I wanted.

You see, I was ambitious in the limited way of domestic servants and just as I'd seen when I started that it would be better to cook food for the rich rather than clear up their mess, I now realised it would be better to be in charge in the kitchen rather than be the skivvy. I also thought that I would try to be nice to the skivvy who might work for me – though the kitchen maids who worked under me later on would probably tell you a different story.

The problem is that when you become cook you worry too much and get stressed that things won't come out right and it makes you crotchety. If things don't come out right then cook is the first to hear about it and one bad meal could lead to the sack, so you end up living on your nerves.

But that was in the future and for now I was just in the mood to find another job and determined at last to get into the big city – well, Norwich at least.

I loved the countryside as a child but blow me down it was dull for a young woman back then. A few dances there might have been here and there but how was I to get to them? There were hardly any buses and I didn't have a bicycle. I still loved painting and drawing but I wanted a bit more of life. Norwich was the answer. Of course I could have gone to London but everyone who ever told me anything about London said that any girl who went there would be corrupted – ruined as they used to put it – within five minutes. It was just sin from one end of town to the other – or that's what we were told.

I could have done with a bit of sin by then, I can tell you! I was in my twenties and had never been properly kissed or anything and my only sense of being attractive came through that poisonous old goat Mr Mayes.

So Norwich was going to be the answer to all my problems. I'd find a man and lots of interesting things to do. Well, I did get to Norwich in the end and I did at last meet a young man but it ended in sadness.

I got my chance to go to Norwich through the local

paper. I found a job advertised for a cook – it was definitely a cook this time, I made sure of that – and wrote an application in my best handwriting. A few days later I received a reply asking me to go for an interview. Mrs Warren was lovely when I told her that I was thinking of leaving. There was none of that horrible business of taking a week's money just because I needed time for an interview. I was amazed when she started to cry and said she would be sorry to see me go and that Daisy, my predecessor, had gone for the same reason.

'What was that?' I said

'Oh, all the drunken swearing and shouting,' she said.

'I don't mind a bit about that,' I replied. 'I know he's harmless just as you said. I'm only moving because I want a bit of life before I'm an old maid. I want to live in the city for a bit just to see what it's like.'

This was a bit of a fib really. I did find all that swearing and shouting a bit off-putting. But I didn't want to upset Mrs Warren.

It meant a lot to me that we'd part as friends.

She let me have time off for the interview and when I showed my new employer my book of recipes and explained how I'd been learning on the job they told me that I could have the job there and then. I always think I must have come across as a reliable sort at interviews because I always seemed to get offered any job I went for. Maybe it was being a solid and healthy-looking country girl that did the trick.

Mrs Warren told me the master would be fine about a reference. She said she had, as she put it, influence with him.

'What do you mean?' I said.

'If he doesn't do as I ask I think he's afraid I'll tell the whole village he's a drunken maniac,' she laughed. 'He also thinks that if he loses me he'll never get anyone else to cook for him.'

So I got my reference and I got my job – and a pay rise. I was now being paid about £40 a year which seemed a fantastic sum to me. I was a bit of an innocent and didn't realise that if I'd had more experience I could have asked for £50 or even £55.

It's always seemed a strange thing to me, but you got paid less if you were a single-handed cook, as we used to say, than if you had a kitchen maid to help. I suppose you got paid for the responsibility of managing the other person. But with help, the job was easier! There wasn't much sense or reason in the world of domestic service, so there we are.

I was to have a kitchen maid under me in the new place, which was an ugly Georgian house – but a big one – in Norwich. The lady who interviewed me really was a lady, the first I'd ever encountered. She was very different from the doctor's wife or the drunk with family money. But at the same time I had a feeling that the family had come down a bit in the world. At my interview she said:

'We used to have a larger staff but I hope you won't mind if you work with one other kitchen staff. The gardener will help with heavier work and of course fruit and vegetables.'

She also asked me the sort of things I could cook and I showed her my book and we went through it together. I think she was a little disappointed I didn't know more but Mrs Spencer had passed on enough French recipes for me not to look like a complete ignoramus.

Considering I was a farm worker's girl she spoke

rather nicely to me. I wasn't used to it but I'd heard that those with genuine breeding never really look down at the poor. They don't patronise or pity them either. They would no more dream of befriending a poor person or inviting them round for dinner than of flying to Mars but at least you felt it was straight talking with none of that jumped-up sneering. I much preferred my new situation to working for rich old farmers or doctors desperate to seem more upper class than they really were.

So I got on well with her ladyship from the first day and that continued all the years I worked for her, which was from the mid 1930s until the late 1940s – all through the Second World War in fact.

Every day in my early years she would come down to the kitchen promptly at nine in the morning, knock and then enter. I would wait for her standing by the smaller of the two kitchen tables which always had a white table-cloth on it. When she came in she would say, 'Good morning, Mrs Jackman' – even unmarried cooks were always 'Mrs' – and sit down as delicately as you can imagine. I never tried to copy her airs and graces although a lot of servants were tempted by that sort of thing, which is why you often heard butlers with slightly affected voices – half Eton and half Norfolk! I always felt sorry for people who felt they had to do that, so I spoke even broader Norfolk when I was in the presence of the quality as we used to call them,

When I say my new employer had airs and graces I don't mean it nastily because I think they came naturally to her. I was a farm girl so I sat down (after her) like a farm girl. She sort of floated into the chair with a hiss of silk. She had the look of someone able to keep as much of herself as possible apart from anything in the kitchen except the air she had to breathe and the chair she had to sit on.

She had a slightly Spanish look I thought, very dark and handsome, with her hair always up, but loosely and sort of swept round and up the sides of her face. I used to chuckle inwardly because while we talked – and the conversation never lasted longer than two minutes – she'd look around as if amazed to find herself in such an odd place as the kitchen. I used to think, Well it might look a bit rough to you but this is where everything you eat is cooked!

She'd tell me what she wanted to eat. She was far keener on exotic recipes than my previous employers. I had my French recipes of course but she also had a pile of sheets showing recipes she liked so I copied those into my book. There was also the house book where lots of recipes had been added over the years.

Most recipes then were based on seasonal food as there were no fridges and apart from bananas and oranges (which disappeared completely during the war) not much was imported.

The most amazing thing I have to confess about this house is that in all the years I worked there I never got a good look round. I think I probably only saw about a third of it at most. The reason was that there were several housemaids, my kitchen maid who was called Daisy, a butler and a footman, gardener, parlourmaid and a boy who did odd jobs.

With all those staff there were strict rules about where you could go. Kitchen staff – even the cook – were only allowed where they had to be to work. Housemaids did come in the kitchen now and then, but they were only allowed to be in the parts of the house where they were supposed to be when working. So they could go in the bedrooms mid morning and in the day rooms early before breakfast but not at any other time, and it was a sacking offence to get caught in the wrong place at the wrong time.

The cook – even a relatively junior cook such as I was at this time – had a certain status in the house because it was common knowledge that good cooks were getting harder to find. Girls were starting to think the long years of apprenticeship as kitchen maid were just too awful even if at the end of it you became a cook and the mistress of the house was a bit more respectful to you.

Chapter Thirty-Two

Was it really worth it? I still thought it was better to cook for them than to clear up for them but the world was full of bitter middle-aged-and-older cooks who'd wasted all their lives in the kitchens of the rich. Even if you weren't a complete mug who meekly accepted all the rules and the lack of time off, you still had little chance of a life outside unless you were really lucky and married someone who was also in service. To get permission to do that you had to bow and scrape and accept that, if you were a woman, you would immediately on marrying lose your job.

Skivvying all the hours that God sends hadn't been a lot of fun, but I'd done it because I knew it would lead to the status of a cook's job. But once I was there and at last a full-time cook who dealt directly with the mistress of the house I was disappointed. It wasn't what I thought it would be. You had to get it right three or four meals a day, every day, year in and year out, and you could never blame anyone but yourself if a complaint came down from the family about the quality of the food. And complaints did come now and then though thankfully not so often that I felt I should give it up.

* * *

My new Norwich house took a bit of getting used to. It was easily the grandest I'd worked in so far. I can still see its two sturdy pillars, one on either side of the huge front door, and the long rows of windows on three floors above. The windows on the ground floor on either side of the front door went down almost to the ground and it was here, in the ballroom, that dances were sometime held, for which of course I did the cooking.

The kitchen was twice the size of anything I'd been in before. In fact it was pretty much twice the size of any room of any kind I'd ever been in with a ceiling maybe fourteen feet high and huge windows. The devices and pots and pans in their range and complexity were amazing. It was as if the Victorians – and this was really still a Victorian kitchen – wanted to make everything as complicated as possible. The amount of equipment was incredible and I'm sure it was like that only because there were so many staff in a typical big house in Victorian times. People perhaps only looked at simplifying things when they were forced to, when servants were suddenly hard to come by and even the rich had to make do with one or two or even none at all.

Apart from all the pots and pans and plates and cutlery which most people would recognise we had leather-covered plate boards and leather-covered knife-cleaning boards. Knives were washed in soapy water and then rubbed on the leather board until they gleamed. Then there was a fork-cleaning device which looked like a big comb, a knife sharpener that looked like a big old milk churn and countless cleaning brushes designed to do all sorts of ridiculous jobs. There were tapered brushes and curved brushes, long, short, round, square and oblong brushes that their makers pretended had a specific use, though of course they didn't at all. Most could have been used for any cleaning job. There were jug brushes, plate brushes, saucepan brushes, wallpaper brushes, floor brushes, hearth brushes, skirting-board brushes, rug brushes and even celery bloody brushes!

Other equipment came in similar quantities. There were at least five different types and sizes of sieve. There were fish kettles, egg and milk pans, soup pots, asparagus boilers and all sorts of silly specialist jars and casseroles.

And there stood the cook in the middle of it all. In my case I stood there with poor Daisy, both of us working fourteen- and often sixteen-hour days. Half the time was spent cleaning up and rehanging all the masses of pots and pans we used, and the other half broiling and roasting, chopping and blending, sieving and mashing.

Chapter Thirty-Three

One night I was exhausted and very hot because we'd been cooking masses of stuff all day for a party. I stepped out for a minute to get some air. I kept at the back of the house and heard the sound of music and an occasional shout of laughter. I felt curiosity get the better of me so I sneaked round to the front. There was no moon so little danger of being seen. I crept through the bushes until I could see the long windows of the ballroom and I was amazed at what I saw.

There must have been fifteen or twenty couples dancing and drinking and the doors were open on to the garden. It was a reminder of how different we really were, the rich and the poor.

I saw the glamorous dresses and the bright lights and heard music I'd never heard before. I'd never danced in my life. I must admit I felt very sorry for myself when I slipped back round the house and into the kitchen. It just didn't seem fair that all the fun should be allocated by luck, by the mere fact of being born into wealth. But seeing that party strengthened my resolve to get a life for myself before it was too late. I knew I would always need to work but I still had my dream of a house of my own. I'd been saving – which wasn't that difficult because I had so little leisure time to spend any money I earned, and my parents, God bless them, had long ago told me they didn't need my money. I hardly ever saw them now but wrote occasionally. My father had retired but been allowed to stay in his cottage in return for a few odd jobs – his arthritis was too bad to allow him to continue to plough.

Chapter Thirty-Four

Relationships always seemed to me such strange things. I got on very well with Daisy, my kitchen maid, but we were not close – well, not at first. I had no boyfriend and was beginning to feel a bit of an old maid.

One sad incident occurred after I'd been in the Norwich house for about two years. One of the grand-children – a little boy of about six – used to come to stay and when he did I would be asked to bake a cake, several cakes, as well as biscuits and extra puddings, especially if he stayed for a few weeks or the whole summer.

The little boy began to come down to the kitchen to chatter, asking for things to eat at odd times and to finish off any cake mix left in the mixing bowls.

Now servants always had a really tricky time knowing how to behave with the young children of the families they worked for. By ten or twelve they would have cottoned on that they were a race apart from the servants and would behave towards us pretty much as their parents – or in this case grandparents – behaved, but younger than that and they were often not aware of the rules. This little boy was definitely not aware of the rules.

The first few times he ran in to the kitchen he just smiled and said hello. He seemed very sweet to me. He came down once or twice more and asked a few polite questions. He was always very polite. Then one afternoon he came down when we were making cakes so I gave him a bowl that we'd been mixing some sweet stuff in.

I didn't want to seem overfamiliar in case he went straight back upstairs and started saying that we'd been talking to him. Beyond an occasional hello this would be frowned on. But with the bowl on his knees he just chatted away, licked the bowl clean and then trotted off back upstairs. But after that he came more often and would stay and talk and ask about the kitchen. I had to be polite while being careful not to overdo it. He always behaved very naturally and after a bit I rather liked having him in the kitchen. He stayed longer and longer and came more often as the summer wore on and I deliberately found things for him to eat that I knew he would like – bits of chocolate and cake and so on. He was incredibly talkative but in the most lovely way. I wish I could remember more of the sort of things he would say, but one that used to make me laugh was that if he liked something – and he nearly always did – he would say, 'Oh conkers, this is delicious.' He made the days much more fun I must say and I grew very fond of him. He had to wear a very uncomfortable-looking suit a lot of the time and was always pulling at the collar. One day he said: 'Can I take this off a bit? It's a bugger.' I was so amazed that I forgot myself and laughed and he immediately beamed at me and started to laugh too. It was one of those little moments when you know that it really didn't matter who you were or where you came from if you could share a joke. Of course I should probably have been a bit stern or at least avoided laughing but the way he said it was so funny you'd have had to be made of stone not to smile.

He used to come down, knock, wait a bit and then peer round the kitchen door – and he had a lovely head of brown curls that always appeared round the door before his face. He would say, 'May I come in, Mrs Cook?' which I thought was very polite. He'd then say, 'I don't suppose you have anything sweet I could just try?' This politeness was the thing we were surprised by and Daisy used to stand there with her mouth open when he spoke to us. Several times I went over to her and pushed her chin back up!

But it all ended in tears as such things always did in those days. He came down one day, sat on a stool we kept by the edge of the range and started to tell us that he had found a toad or something equally exciting in the garden. Before he could ask I said, 'Would you like some hot chocolate?' He smiled his big happy smile and nodded.

After he had finished his chocolate and stayed talking for half an hour he said goodbye in his usual way. Then, just as he started to walk over to the door to the stairs, he ran back to me and put his arms round my waist and gave me a hug. After that he never came down again and I found out later from one of the housemaids that he had been scolded for coming down to see us.

Wasn't that terrible? And so sad. I used to think about it for ages afterwards and even forty years on it was something that came into my mind now and then and I wondered what sort of man he had become and if he remembered me. I was so upset not to see him again. He was only a child and we were hardly going to corrupt him, but I think he'd overstepped the mark by being too friendly. Perhaps he mentioned us and his visits to us to his family. I suspect his parents were horrified. For them it would have been a crime against the natural order. It was as if the local landowner's son had been caught playing with the common boys from the village. It wasn't supposed to happen.

But it must have been a shock for the little boy too. I mean a shock to discover that his innocent little visits to the kitchen were somehow shaming. I think he didn't get much attention from his parents. That's why he came down and that's why he gave me a hug. I loved listening to him and I think he could sense it. Back upstairs he had lots of toys, I should imagine, and played with them alone. That old saw about children being seen and not heard. They probably believed that if you hugged a little boy it would make him soft or some such nonsense.

Chapter Thirty-Five

The house where all this happened so long ago was, as I say, a big house, but I always thought it was quite boring to look at. It was very plain. It had a long drive that swept round the front of the house and then out again making a circle round an area of grass and dense shrubs and trees. The trees had grown so high that the front of the house always seemed to be in shadow. The house also had a very complicated internal arrangement that used to fox me even after a decade and more.

It had three sets of stairs: the main stairs for the family, the servants' stairs at the back and another set at one end that only went halfway up the house, but if you went down it took you to the cellars.

The basement extended out further than the walls of the house above, and down there passages ran to the old wine cellars and other storerooms and an ice house. I wouldn't have wandered along those passages at night for a hundred pounds. The whole house had an odd, gloomy feel to it inside and although we servants all used the tradesmen's entrance and were forbidden to go snooping around, I did get a look once or twice at the hall and the main reception rooms which were enormous and very grand – or at least they looked so to me.

I noticed the furniture was a little shabby and the house hadn't been decorated in years, and it was never decorated in my time there. The coal fires had yellowed many of the walls, particularly those above the big marble fireplaces. The truth is I think that grand though they were, the family was a bit short of money – which is why her ladyship had said at my interview that they had previously had a larger staff. I suspect it was also why they took on a relatively inexperienced cook: I was cheaper than a French chef.

But I didn't mind. Looking back I realise that my great ambition to be a cook and own my own house would seem like very small beer to any intelligent girl born later than me. But at the time poor girls knew they couldn't aspire to much. We hadn't the education. Being a schoolteacher would have seemed as remote to me as being a high court judge.

I'd become a cook but being a cook had as many disadvantages as advantages.

The truth is that though I didn't like being bossed around it turned out I liked it even less when it was my turn to boss someone else around. I just wasn't cut out for it. I hated the fact that I had to get Daisy, the kitchen maid, to go faster or do things differently and when we were under pressure, which was often, I hated the fact that I wasn't as nice to her as I should have been. I shouted because I was terrified that I would get it wrong myself and that her ladyship would criticise or at worst ask me to leave.

I had nothing to fall back on without a job. Both my mother and father were old and ill now and I was very much on my own with no brothers or sisters to turn to either. So I had to make it work.

Chapter Thirty-Six

In the great house I had my own room and not in the attic. It was at the back of the house and although it was in the basement, at least technically, the ground at the back of the house was lower than at the front so my room had two windows looking on to a small part of the garden. I had my own fire – made each day by one of the housemaids – and a bigger bed than I'd ever hoped to have. I had a desk, bookcase, mirror and even a sofa. It had been the housekeeper's room but unusually for the time they had decided not to have a housekeeper. I assumed again that they were beginning to feel the pinch and had to save money. I never got to sleep late in the mornings, but at least my bed was comfortable and I was big enough now to look after myself so if anyone had sneaked in and tried to climb into bed with me they'd have got a punch on the nose!

Daisy was a lovely girl and I know she never held my occasional bouts of bad temper against me. One of the things I learned to love about her was her sense of fun. As soon as I got a bit tetchy she'd make some joke or other or start her funny mumbling or she'd make a pretend horrified sort of face at me and say, 'Don't hit me, Mother!' We always made it up anyway and I gave her more time off than she should have had and we started buying each other presents. We were like best friends at school.

As she was quite new I gave her the advice I'd been given all those years ago and the advice I gave to every kitchen maid – that she should keep a book and write down everything I told her about the way to cut vegetables for various dishes, how to make soufflés (everyone was obsessed with bloody soufflés in those days), quenelles and all the other things you needed to know if you were to progress to be a cook.

But after a while I realised that domestic service wasn't the only thing she planned to do with her life. I felt a pang of envy when she said she hoped to get a job in a factory in a year or two. I'd never really thought of that and it shows how narrow my upbringing was: I'd always been taught that factories were inferior to domestic service and here was someone telling me they were much better. But Daisy was a Norwich girl, a town girl, and at half my age knew twice as much about the world as I did. And of course the world was changing. Even I knew that. Daisy and other younger maids I met were more confident now. I could tell they were less prepared to put up with what us old girls had been saddled with! We caught the last of the old Victorian world of total deference. They caught the beginning of the new world where you could choose. And the truth is I wanted to be with the new world not the old.

When Daisy wanted to come back really late from a dance on Wednesday or on her Saturday evening off, I used to leave the door open. I'd have been in a lot of trouble if I'd been caught doing this, but just because I'd had so little dancing fun and never been to a party I didn't see why she should suffer in the same way. And she was so full of life it was impossible not to want to make her smile. Having said that she could be horribly clumsy and she often dropped dishes of food on the floor, or she'd trip over something and fall on her face, but I used to say to her:

'Daisy, when we get busy and I'm at my wits' end you know I'm going to shout at you again, but you must take no notice. Don't be upset because I have to let off steam – but don't you dare shout back!'

'Yes, Dolly,' she would reply. Why she called me Dolly I have no idea but it made me laugh and I didn't mind.

'I'm Mrs Jackman to you, or Cook,' I used to say.

'Yes, Dolly, of course you are,' she'd reply. 'But how about Mrs Cook or Dolly Cook?' and I'd then take a swipe at her with the dishcloth.

Daisy was a bit like me. She was from a very poor background. Her father was a labourer who did day-work in the city; but despite that she was ambitious and fearless. She had about as much education as me but she wanted to go places and she had a sort of courage I know I lacked. I think that made me feel a bit maternal towards her. She was terrifically skinny, which was a contrast to my increasing bulk.

One unusual thing I discovered when telling Daisy how to get into the house late at night without being noticed was that the builders had included what was called a 'trick step' on the wooden treads of the servants' stairs.

Daisy had to go right to the top of the stairs to get to her room and I told her that about four steps up from the bottom the step was about two inches higher than the others. The idea was that a burglar (or a late servant!) creeping up the stairs would trip up and fall and wake the house up and get caught, or having made a noise would quickly make his escape. But I could just see Daisy tripping on the step – she was an expert at tripping anyway – and then we'd all be in trouble.

I should say a bit more about Daisy as she's important in my story. She made my job so much easier after our early difficult start and she brightened up the days.

After she got the hang of what I needed for the various meals we had to prepare she would have the salt and pepper, the various cutting boards and dishes and utensils in place every day almost without me saying a word. Some weeks she would guess what we'd need before I told her. It was part of her charm you see – she seemed a bit flighty and dizzy but was really very practical underneath it all.

And even when I was reaching the end of my tether because we were under pressure for a dinner party or whatever she would stay calm. Like so many of us girls then she could hardly write a good letter, but she had what I called native intelligence and bags of it.

She was also a bit of a comic and did a wonderful turn pretending to be a great dancer such as Isadora Duncan or one of the famous actresses of the day. I always knew when she was going to start her antics. I'd be concentrating on stirring a sauce such as hollandaise that would go wrong in an instant if you didn't concentrate and out of the corner of my eye I'd see her starting to sway her hips and look up to heaven like a great romantic heroine and of course I'd start to giggle. It was impossible not to. Then she'd do a ridiculous but very accurate imitation of the mistress discussing the food in a voice like the queen and then switch suddenly into very rough cockney.

She'd say, 'I really think that the endives need more *je ne sais quoi* . . . The little bastards need a kick in their feckin' arse that's what they feckin' need.' Or, 'My lady's bastard fishcake is to be presented at court this year. Tarts are on the house.'

That was a favourite little phrase of hers and I never really worked out if it meant anything!

It was so funny that I had to get quite angry with her sometimes in case the food was ruined, but now I wish I could remember more of what she said. She always knew when to stop and she'd wink at me and concentrate wonderfully on her work for a while until the next bout of high jinks.

But despite her ambition she never left for that factory job. She did something much better instead.

Chapter Thirty-Seven

On my Wednesday evenings and odd weekends off, I used to get the bus into the town centre and just have a look round. Norwich seemed huge to me and I was always getting lost. In those days there were no modern buildings and the narrow medieval alleys and streets seemed to lead back and forth and in and out till you didn't know where you were.

I went to the old Astoria cinema a few times and to the Alexander but I always felt slightly sad having to go on my own at the weekends when there were always other girls going in with their boyfriends. You see I felt a bit of an old maid by this time. What you've never had you never miss, I used to say to myself (though not completely believing it). And although I was really fond of Daisy and though she probably would have come out with me, mixing together outside work would have been frowned on. But never mind. Despite the difficulties, Daisy was to play a big part in my life later on.

I thought about why I didn't get much attention from men. I supposed it was inevitable because I spent most of my time in other people's kitchens and also I knew I wasn't the most attractive girl in the world, but I used to think, Your time will come, girl, and if all else fails you can get a bloody cat!

I still had my painting and drawing of course. I remember going to an artists' materials shop in Norwich and buying some really good watercolours and the best art paper I could get. Oh, I was so pleased with myself and then I thought on later days off I'd find a church or square to paint, because before the war and the bombs Norwich was a lovely place.

And it was through painting that my time did come. It was through painting that I met Charlie the copper, as I liked to call him. Charlie was the first, but sadly not the last of my short list of admirers.

I remember I had walked quite a way about the town one day before deciding where to paint. I'd finally settled down on a little stool I carried with me in the church-yard of St James Pockthorpe. Pockthorpe itself, I mean that part of the town round the church, was quite a rough area, but St James was a lovely old church with a strange-shaped tower. It was a Sunday, after the service had ended, and a lovely spring day. I was painting but feeling a little uncomfortable because I didn't really think I was an artist at all, as I wasn't trained in any way. I always worried that people would come across and have a look and think, She can't paint at all.

But I felt I had to paint, you see, so I put up with the risk that people would judge me and in the end I usually became completely absorbed in what I was doing so it didn't matter anyway.

So there I was in my prim servant's hat and woollen coat and not looking even slightly like an artist or a young attractive art student, when a policeman walked straight across the churchyard towards me. In those days when you saw a copper heading your way you always thought you were in trouble. I thought, Oh Christ, I'm trespassing. I'm for it now!

Well he came up to me and said, 'Are you all right, love?'

I said, 'Of course I'm all right.' Which sounded a bit shirty, but I smiled at the same time as he seemed to be worried about me rather than trying to catch me out.

'It's a bit rough round here,' he said. 'You want to watch it.'

'Oh I'll be all right,' I said in my best big-confident-woman voice and carried on with my little picture, which was balanced on my lap as I didn't have an easel.

Well, that was when I began to think something was up because I could see him out of the corner of my eye and he was just standing there.

'That's a lovely thing you've got there,' he said and when I looked up again he was skewing his head round to have a look at my picture. 'Professional artist are you?' he said.

At that I started to laugh and he joined in. He was a round-faced jolly chap who I thought was about thirty though I later discovered he was only twenty-seven.

Then he said, 'I'm off duty tomorrow so if you're here again perhaps we could have a cup of tea.'

There I was, already well over thirty and an old maid by the standards of the day and never been asked out by a boy and then I get asked out by a copper. Well, I couldn't believe my ears. I wasn't the shy type though I hadn't seen much of the world and I thought, Well, better give it a go, Mrs Cook, as it might be the only chance you'll get!

As I had the whole weekend off — which was rare

enough – I thought, Why not? I'd been on my own for far too long and had never been to a dance or for a night of fun and he seemed nice enough. I also thought that if he didn't turn up I'd lost nothing anyway.

So I said, 'All right then. I'll be here at two o clock. Thank you very much.'

Well blow me down, next day he did turn up and, what's more, he had changed. I didn't recognise him. I was sitting in exactly the same place as before but pretending to concentrate on my painting (I was nervous and wasn't concentrating at all) and when a slim man approached me across the churchyard I thought, Here's another one after me. I must have turned into a princess overnight! But lo and behold it was Charlie, my copper, looking much slimmer and younger in his civvies.

So there we are. Waiting had paid off and the cook had her man at last. We went for a cup of tea in a nearby café after he'd said some nice things about my painting and he insisted on paying. Almost all men did back then – they'd have been deeply insulted if you'd insisted on paying even half each. Of course the bad side of that was that, for example, women found their husbands were deeply insulted if they asked them to change a nappy or take the baby out in the pram.

Anyway, Charlie was a very solid no-nonsense type. In fact he was the happiest man I think I ever met. Talk about the laughing policeman! He loved joking and he was good at it, at least when he was off duty. On our second outing he showed me he could do a cartwheel while smoking a cigarette and another time he turned up wearing a big black cape and a wide-brimmed hat just to make me jump. 'I thought you'd like to see me dressed as an artist,' he said with a grin.

The only time I recall him being serious was when he told me about his work. He liked walking the beat, he said, and made a point of talking to anyone he passed along the way. But he hated court work and said he'd never forgotten the time he'd helped arrest an eighteen-year-old who had murdered his mother in a silly argument over whether he should be allowed to stay out late with his friends.

The eighteen-year-old was a nice lad, Charlie said. In a moment of madness he had just lost his temper. Charlie said he'd been in court when the judge put his black cap on and pronounced the death sentence.

The boy had just stared ahead from the dock and clearly hadn't realised that he had just been told he was going to die. In those days there was no genuine appeals system – unless you were well connected – and the boy was duly hanged. Charlie said he had never been able to stop thinking about it. Once or twice a week the boy's face would come into his head either in his dreams or while he was walking the beat. It would be one of the reasons that in the end made him resign from the force. He used to say, 'What really upsets me is that if his father had been a duke he'd have got off with prison almost certainly. I've seen it many times. The judges are always sympathetic to their own sort.'

Over the next few months we went out together. We went to tea shops and for walks because that was the sort of exciting thing you did in Norwich back then. He even came window-shopping for clothes with me a few times. That was very unusual in a man.

Charlie wanted to know all about domestic service. Most men didn't want you at all if they found out you were a servant. But not Charlie. He loved everyone and was interested in everything. In a way I think he even liked the people he had to arrest. He told me about a number of criminals he'd nicked several times over the years. He chased one bloke out of Norwich station after he'd pinched a suitcase and as they ran down a side street the thief looked back and then came to a halt.

When Charlie ran up he said, 'Morning, Charlie, I thought it was you. I didn't want to give you a heart attack so I thought I'd better stop.' Charlie told me he was so delighted he nearly let the chap off.

Once or twice when he'd arrested youngsters he would say to them:

'Look, if I nick you it will be on your record for the rest of your life so I'm not going to nick you. I'm not supposed to do it but I'm going to let you go and we'll say no more about it. But when I see you about the streets I'll expect a wave and a smile and if you wave and smile I'll know you're not getting into trouble. If you don't wave and smile I'm going to nick you.'

Wasn't that a marvellous way to carry on?

He told me it worked a treat and he was so pleased that he'd probably saved a number of young lads from getting into serious crime.

Charlie lodged in a terrace house in Norwich. We never dared go. He used to make hilarious jokes about his landlady, who sounded a terrible old dragon.

'Guess what I had for breakfast,' he used to say.

'What did you have?'

'Two slices of the last lodger!'

Charlie really pepped up my Sundays off though I hardly ever saw him on my half-day as there wasn't enough time. I was never quite sure he really would have liked to see me more. I hope he would have liked to. I think men were more secretive back then. They would never really tell you what they thought about. They thought it was soppy to talk about feelings or love. It was the way they were brought up. Such a pity.

Lovely though Charlie was he hardly told me anything about his childhood or his family and he used to get gloomy if I asked too much. I found out later that both his brothers had died very young and his father had left the family.

'It's not a happy subject,' he used to say. 'I much prefer to stick to the here and now.' And he would smile. I sometimes think that he made so many jokes and liked a lark so much because it took him away from all those memories.

But despite the fact that he found it hard to talk about his feelings we did get to the holding-hands stage and then blow me down but I started to find it all a little embarrassing. I thought I was too old for that teenage hand-holding stuff.

If you were in your thirties back then you were considered old, especially if you were a woman and unmarried. You had to toughen yourself not to feel a failure because it was assumed that every woman – even servants – wanted to be married. It was a big failure, a humiliation really, not to be married. After women's lib girls didn't have to get married at all and there's nothing wrong and no one would dream of judging or criticising. That's how it should always have been.

But I must admit I was old-fashioned. What else could I be back then? I would have liked to be wed and I would have married Charlie but things didn't work out in the end.

Mind you – and I've never told anyone this before

– we did manage to have sex a few times. By the time I was an old woman I thought, well, why did we ever make so much of a fuss about it back then? Why were we so terrified and so ignorant?

By the time I'd grown old everyone young seemed to be having sex the way we had cups of tea and I don't want them thinking I never tried it!

So we put on our best clothes – which in my case didn't amount to much – and went to a hotel on the other side of Norwich and signed in as Mrs and Mrs Jones or something equally silly. I think they were a bit suspicious but what could they do? We were hardly two kids were we, and Charlie being a policeman he knew how to put on a sort of serious air that made people wary of questioning anything he said or did.

Anyway, I laughed for about an hour when Charlie explained what we were going to do! He was lovely about it and even he admitted he had only done it a few times himself with a former girlfriend who, like everyone then, was terrified of getting pregnant. I told him I was petrified too and he said we'd be all right because he had a condom.

Now I had no idea what a condom was and when he told me I thought I would have to be taken to hospital suffering from hysterical laughing. Ridiculous enough that a man has to put *that* in *there* but to put a balloon on it first – that really took the biscuit.

The best thing about sex for me was being close to someone after all those years of sleeping alone in cold beds. I hadn't had that physical closeness since I was a child.

Among the best of Charlie's stories and one he first told me in that hotel bedroom was a great joke about being a cook. I've always remembered because he loved telling it to me – again and again! I have a feeling it was a well-known joke and I was probably the last to hear it but it made me laugh. Young people won't get the joke unless they know that the word copper was slang for pennies and ha'pennies before decimalisation. Here's how Charlie used to tell his favourite joke:

'There's a cook down in a basement of the house and one evening her two nephews – both policemen – call in for a cup of tea. Now strictly speaking this isn't allowed at all but the cook has got away with it for years so doesn't worry much, and besides they were both respectable guardians of the law.

'The mistress never comes down into the kitchen in the afternoons so she'll never know and the cook likes to hear all the goings-on round about from the nephews. And besides, the two nephews only stay for twenty minutes while they have their tea. But on this day there's no change for the gas meter, which takes pennies, and upstairs the mistress of the house realises that the light will soon go out so she opens the door at the top of the stairs and shouts down to the cook:

"Do you have any coppers down there?"

Terrified and all in a fluster of guilt, Cook shouts out:

"I do but don't worry, they're my relatives!"'

I managed to keep seeing Charlie for almost two years – always with the worry that the family would find out and I'd be in trouble. But in 1939 he packed the force in. He also wanted to join the army.

'War is definitely coming,' he said, 'and I want to see the world and get off the beat. I can spend my whole life tramping the streets of Norwich. If I join up I'll be better off than if I get called up and if I don't do it now, before the war starts, I'll be stuck because the police is bound to be a reserved occupation.'

If only he'd known how silly it was to try to go to war. I was so cross with him but I never said a word because I didn't want to upset him or fall out with him. And besides he was one of those men it was impossible to be cross with because he was so charming and always so good-tempered and happy – even about going off to fight. But, oh! I thought he was a silly chump.

When the war started in September of 1939 and I saw the children of the rich going off to Ireland in their droves to avoid the call-up – it made me so mad. But Charlie had a romantic idea of the army. He used to look forward to being with his comrades-in-arms, as he used to say.

At the time I thought he was half mad and half a hero and besides I could never have persuaded him to stay in the police. So off he went and within a few months we were at war. Before he went he agreed – I think to cheer me up because I was so sad at him going – that we should get engaged, so we did and at least I had that.

We wrote to each other now and then after he went away but the letters almost made me miss him more. It was the worst time of my life and Daisy and the others in the house would have been amazed I'm sure to see big old Cook lying in bed at night weeping over Charlie.

After the war really got going he was in France and I sent him a little painting I did of us in the churchyard at Norwich, but I never had a reply to say if he liked it or not, because he was killed a few weeks later.

* * *

At least we didn't have a chance to fall out with each other or for things between us to get bitter with old age, which often happens. It's a terrible thing to say in some ways I know but it has comforted me all down the years. You see, all my memories of Charlie are of him as a young man smiling and of what a lot of fun he was, and that's how I like to remember him. We hadn't known each other long enough to have arguments or to get bored or go off with other people. So it was short but very sweet.

Chapter Thirty-Eight

Back at the house the start of war made little impact at first. Domestic servants were such a hidden army that I thought all those keepers and gardeners would be overlooked for the call-up. The government would hardly know they existed. They might not have cared much about them in peacetime – they certainly didn't care how they were treated by their employers or how little they got paid – but as soon as war began they were very interested in them indeed.

So after a while the men began to disappear and either the gardens became untidy or very old men long retired came back to work. Butlers and footmen disappeared too and not many would come back to their old jobs if they survived the war. They'd seen too much of life and didn't want to get back into the narrow little world they'd come from.

But I stayed on, which is what women did. We didn't have to fight in the war, it's true, but staying at home wasn't all roses.

I hung my pictures in my room and even paid to have a few framed – wasn't that vain of me! And as food shortages got slowly worse I gradually sensed that the family were beginning to rely on Daisy and me in a way they never had before. I didn't get a pay rise for five years but then got another £10 a year at a time when people, even the rich, were shorter of money than they'd ever been.

I was very experienced by now. None of those complicated meals bothered me in the least and the mass of kitchen implements seemed a simple matter to organise. I used to look back and wonder why when I started as a kitchen maid it had all seemed so daunting. I was terrific now at whatever was asked of me, even if I say so myself. The family had to put up with rationing like the rest of us, and to be fair to them they rarely complained when the food was cooked with margarine rather than butter or when the meat was stringy and served up in smaller quantities. But the steady routine of the days was occasionally disrupted and there were bouts of silliness that nearly drove me out, such as the time the family had a big party one winter towards the end of the war.

Her ladyship turned up in the kitchen on the morning of the party in the usual way, giving her polite knock before coming in. We knew each other well by now but she still called me Mrs Jackman. She explained that there were to be twenty to dinner – usually there were five or six so this was a bit of a challenge.

She asked for a few things that were in my book but that we didn't have often because they were so laborious to make. With rabbit quenelles poor Daisy had to push the rabbit through two, sometimes three sieves before the meat was considered fine enough. Personally, I thought it made it into baby food! I thought then and still think now that it is a stupid recipe. I suppose rabbit was one of the few meats readily available during the war and people would try anything to make it more interesting. Through all my years of cooking I thought most fancy recipes were just silly ways to mess about with food – but I never told her ladyship that!

It was winter and we had a lot of game in winter because his lordship was a keen shot. He liked pheasant shooting and went out pretty much every Saturday and Wednesday, I think. He also liked wildfowling – shooting ducks and geese – out on the Norfolk and Lincolnshire marshes. As a result I had to deal with a lot of what you might call unusual birds: snipe, plover, different types of geese and now and then woodcock.

On the day of the big party her Ladyship told me to expect woodcock, which was considered a great delicacy by the gentry.

Now the woodcock and the way you cook and eat it is one of the most disgusting things known to man, but if it was hard to get hold of and complicated to cook the quality were bound to want to eat it. That's what I always thought.

The big day started when I got up extra early along with Daisy and we worked our way over the kitchen checking all the pots and pans carefully to make sure everything was ready.

The point of this was that we both knew that generally, if the family were unhappy with a particular meal, they would not make too much of a fuss. They knew that the other days of the year you'd cook well for them. But when there were important guests the family feared they would be looked down on and gossiped about if the cook produced a bad meal. It sort of lowered the standing of the family, because it meant they couldn't afford a good cook, which at that time meant one from France. While our careful major preparations were going on, I still had to get the breakfast and lunch ready and, of course, I cooked for the other staff too. So that meant two breakfasts and two lunches being cooked at the same time we were getting the quenelles and the woodcock ready. Now you can see why there was hardly time to breathe let alone sit down for a minute or two.

By mid afternoon I was cursing like a navvy or maybe I should say like Daisy. I used to have a laugh with her because she was so hard-working but also so foul-mouthed. I used to say, and I said it on this day, 'You can curse your head off when it gets really hectic if it makes you feel better.' The truth is she had a great line in swearing and it lightened the mood, although I should have been sacked for encouraging her.

On the day of the woodcock dinner she was cutting vegetables, rushing from sink to sink, pouring boiling water into pots and pans and plugholes, and all the while I'd hear her mumbling:

'I hope they choke you, you bastards. Why can't you eat them like any other mortal? Oh, no, you have to have them in little thin strips to drive me to distraction, you black-hearted bastards.'

She'd say much worse than that, too, but I used to laugh and throw a cloth at her if it got really bad. She once ran across the kitchen having burned her hand a bit (it wasn't too serious but it gave her a fright) shouting, 'Fuck, fuck, fuck, fuck!'

I wish I could convey the comic way she had of saying such things – but it's so difficult. She'd hop across the room sticking her tongue out, half amused and half in agony. It was such a comic turn!

Chapter Thirty-Nine

In many houses the staff got far worse food than the family but I wasn't having any of that and as I was in charge of deliveries from the local shops I had my way. I knew the staff were far too sensible to want those bloody woodcock, though.

So that evening – the evening of the woodcock dinner I mean – Daisy and I were cutting and chopping like mad. They wanted five courses which included soup and those dratted woodcock.

The soup was a disgusting enough business. Normally we would put all the bones and gristle and leftover meat in a big pot with a tap at the bottom to drain the liquid off and this liquid would be used to make the soup. After a while all that bone and gristle and slops would begin to stink, especially in summer, but no one worried much about that and we always used it as the basis for soups.

I used to say, 'They'll be having a very high soup today, very high and mighty,' and Daisy would laugh. I would never make such remarks when the butler or footmen appeared because we always saw them as far more on the side of the family. The butlers and foot-men liked to encourage that idea too because it made them feel superior. It was another case, as my father used to say, of tuppence hal'penny looking down on tuppence.

So on the great day we got the soup ready. Once the soup was done and the vegetables prepared that evening, I got down to the woodcock. They are quite boring little brown birds with a long beak and once you've plucked them there's hardly enough meat for a mouthful. You twist the beak round and push it up the bird's bottom! You also didn't draw, that is gut them, like other birds – they were cooked intact – but I worried about them burning so I continually checked them in the oven.

You need at least one woodcock per person and we had ten this night for the five guests. It was a show-off meal so the greedy buggers got two each.

Daisy used to say, 'Who invents these bloody things?'

I said to her, 'What do your boyfriends think of all that swearing of yours?'

'I don't give a stuff,' she said. 'Boyfriends are all bastards too, like these woodcock!'

Soon we were ready and the butler and footman came down to collect the soup on a silver tray. They always wore white gloves – it wasn't to hide their hard-working hands, it was to protect the family from working-class germs, or Germans, which is what Daisy used to call them!

As soon as the soup had gone up we had to get those woodcock ready on a big dish, the poor devils looking up at us out of their poor roasted eyes. Off they went with the butler and his staff and not a word said to us.

But Daisy said, 'I wonder that butler can get round the house at all he's on such a high horse!'

Then, later, pudding and at last we could relax a bit

– though of course for Daisy there was still the washing-up to be done.

I hated going to bed and leaving poor Daisy to finish so I usually made tea while she was scrubbing and scouring and cursing. We usually finished by ten o'clock but tonight we weren't both able to sit down till after midnight. I remember sitting staring at poor Daisy who had tremendously thick dark blonde hair which she shook out almost in relief from under her cap once the last pans had been put away.

She said, 'That was a bugger, wasn't it?'

'It was,' I said. 'Do you want to go to bed?'

'No, I'll wait a while,' said Daisy.

And then something terrible happened. All the colour drained out of Daisy's face and without a word she just sort of slid off the chair on to the hard stone floor. I managed to catch her before the back of her head hit the flagstones and sort of dragged her to a sitting position by the wall. I was so shocked I didn't know what to do. There was no question of waking the family, who would have gone to bed by now, and I hadn't a clue about the nearest doctor. I just sat on the floor next to Daisy and cradled her head. I felt a terrible welling up of tears that I couldn't control. I thought Daisy – who was really my only friend – was going to die there and then. I was paralysed and I've felt bad ever since that I was so useless at the time. After a few minutes she started to come round and when her eyes opened and she saw my scared face just a few inches away, she said, 'If yer planning to kiss me you'd better get on with it!'

I was so relieved that I ended up laughing, crying and half telling her off. She just smiled and I got her back on the chair.

'I haven't done that since I was a child,' she said.

'What haven't you done?'

'I used to faint pretty regular. I'd just keel over. Very useful at school to get out of learning!'

Typical of Daisy to make a joke of something that anyone else might have worried about. It was just stress and exhaustion I think, because she had started work that day at about five. With a fifteen-hour day behind her is it any wonder she fainted?

A message came down the next day saying how much the family and their guests had enjoyed the meal. So fair play to them, they did at least acknowledge when they thought we'd done good work. But when I heard this I couldn't help thinking about those woodcock because there is one thing about them that I haven't mentioned.

If you like eating woodcock, it's not the gamey flavour you're really after. It's not even the fact that this little morsel takes a cook ages to prepare. No. The best bit of the woodcock is the contents of its gut. Here's what you do.

You take a piece of toast and then, when the bird is lying there on your plate you squeeze it down with your knife till the guts ooze out over your toast. It's called woodcock trail and how they loved to eat it. No servant in his or her right mind would dream of eating such a thing!

Another oddity the upper classes liked to eat now and then was rook pie. Young rooks were shot and just the breast meat cut off. They were tricky to cook in such a way that you got rid of the slightly bitter taste. We also had lots of rabbits, as I've said, and hares – poor buggers had to be roasted in a sauce made from their own blood – and venison from Scotland in season.

Because the rabbits arrived at the house in their skins we kept them all – the skins I mean – and they were sold to the rabbit-skin man. Daisy was given the money and she richly deserved it I must say. And this wasn't a tradition in our house only – it happened all over. The kitchen maid or the scullery maid was always given the money paid for the rabbit skins. It was just a few shillings but poor Daisy was paid little enough so it was a nice bonus.

I felt sorry when I heard in the 1950s that almost all the rabbits were gone and rabbit was no longer a popular dish. Some bloody idiot introduced myxomatosis and killed almost all of them. But by then of course the old-fashioned servants had pretty much vanished too, and even at my most optimistic I couldn't see her ladyship pushing rabbit flesh through three increasingly fine sieves!

A few weeks after the big woodcock dinner both Daisy and I saw just how selfish even apparently reasonable employers could be. We spent the day getting a shoot lunch ready. It was complicated because we had to make stews and soups and then put them in big earthenware pots which were then put into wooden boxes and surrounded by hay to keep them warm. They were then loaded into a shooting brake and off they went to the shoot. But while we were getting all this ready we still had to cook lunch for the servants and members of the family who hadn't gone shooting. It was another exhausting day and the returned pots weren't cleaned and put away until nearly midnight. Then, two hours later, I was woken and asked to prepare hot chocolate for various members of the family who had been sitting up playing cards. There was no thought that poor old Cook might be exhausted after her fifteen-hour day.

Honestly, as I made that chocolate, I wanted to spit in it!

Chapter Forty

Our kitchen had no mod cons and also even had one or two strange outdated features. It had a spit jack, for example.

Built with a weight on a pulley, the spit jack had a crude, clock-like series of wheels and gears and with a big weight attached it slowly turned the massive roasting spit above the fire. The weight would take about fifteen minutes to reach the ground and all that time you could get on with other tasks safe in the knowledge that your roasting pig would be evenly cooked on all sides.

The spit was attached to the great beam across the chimney breast. In really big houses they attached the spit to a small wheel and kept a specially trained terrier to run round inside it when the roast need to be turned.

The range, which was a massive thing with several ovens, had to be cleaned regularly and covered in black lead by poor Daisy. It had a small metal door at the back of the chimney on the outside wall where the sweep and his boy would come regularly to clean.

But I can tell you there was real skill in getting the temperatures right in those ovens for various dishes. You did it by trial and error and experience because the primitive heat gauges, when you had them, were so unreliable. On a gas or electric stove, any fool can cook if she follows the recipe, but on those old ranges you needed to know all the peculiarities of your particular range. That's partly why cooks became so valued by the time domestic service had become a choice girls no longer had to make. As the number of cooks went down and the remaining ones got older, the price went up.

Knife grinders still came to the door as well as all the local and not so local traders and shopkeepers. I would buy what we needed – according to what was in season – and keep a tally for her ladyship, although after the first few months she hardly bothered to check anything. And no tradesman would ever ask for money, however long they were kept waiting. They just discreetly left a bill at the end of the week or at the end of the month.

There was a silly idea that the upper classes were not to be troubled by petty financial considerations. The poor old tradesman was made to feel that *he* was the grubby one, concerned with trivia by even asking for payment, despite the fact that the poor man (and his wife and children) relied on the money.

Mind you, if there was the least hint that a family had run out of money – something that did happen in the 1920s and 1930s – the tradesman's habit of deference immediately disappeared and he'd be clamouring at the door for payment.

You see underneath it all the deference was about money and the power it gave you. The upper classes thought the lower orders admired them for their superior qualities, but it wasn't true. The poorer sort didn't admire them at all – all they admired was their cash.

Chapter Forty-One

There was a very friendly grocer who used to come to the house every Monday. This was Mr Murphy and Daisy and I loved it when he came because that man could talk like an angel – I wish I'd been able to write it down. It was charming and eccentric and funny all at the same time.

He'd knock on the door at about nine o clock in the morning and whether Daisy or me opened the door he always said the same thing:

'Is it yourself now, Mrs Jackman?'

I would say, 'Who else would it be?' and if it was Daisy she'd just giggle.

He'd then say something such as, 'Is that a new hairstyle you have there? That's a style of the first class. And either you have been to one of those delicate German spas or the Good Lord is making your skin fresher and younger each time I see you.'

He'd go on like that and at the end of twenty minutes you'd hardly noticed you'd ordered half a ton of stuff from him – and often it was half a ton more than you really wanted.

When I told people later on about old Murphy they'd say, 'Didn't you hate all that old guff and nonsense?'

And I'd say, 'Oh, it was so nicely done you couldn't be offended.'

Of course it was just outrageous flattery. I said to him once, 'You'd flatter the bloody cat if she answered the door.'

It was just an entertaining habit he had and I think in a funny way he really did mean it. And if he didn't it was such fun to listen to that it was hard to mind. It was a bit of entertainment at a dull time of the week.

When I said that about the cat he just smiled, leaned back a bit, stroked his chin and said, 'Is that the fine specimen of a cat I've seen wandering about? That must surely be the best mouser in the country? Am I right?' And even as he said it there was far more than a twinkle in his eye.

Old Murphy was also an eccentric dresser. He'd have a white silk cravat wound about ten times round his neck, a red or canary yellow waistcoat and a billycock hat, like something out of the nineteenth century.

Chapter Forty-Two

When the grouse came in August and September we had to leave them hanging for a couple of weeks in a cool room that had air coming into it from outside. The family didn't like to eat the birds until they were really high.

You knew when they were ready because maggots would be dropping off them in a steady stream. Unless you've cleaned – that is, gutted – a really rotten grouse you can have no idea of the stomach-churning smell. Very few people can do it without retching – even if they do it outside in the fresh air. When I showed Daisy how to do it the first time she really was sick and had to leave the room for a while. The trick is to take very shallow breaths and to do it very quickly, but I'm sure if the family had known the state of the birds as I prepared them they would have thought twice about eating them. Apart from the maggots, their guts would also often be full of what looked like tapeworms – and the worms were still alive.

I used to think, if that's a delicacy you can keep it.

You always knew when it was the game-shooting season in a big house because the lavatories – or so the housemaids told me – were always full of lead shot. It was considered bad form to spit out any lead shot you found in your woodcock or snipe or grouse so you just swallowed it and of course a lot of the birds were absolutely full of tiny pieces of lead shot so it was all going through the guts of the various members of the family and ending up in the toilet where it was too heavy to be flushed away. Give me fish and chips any day.

So that was another terrible cleaning job for the housemaids. I used to think aristocrats were eccentric not because they had nothing to do except order us about, but because they were suffering from lead poisoning. And they probably were.

Chapter Forty-Three

Before she came to me Daisy had worked in a huge country house with the usual kitchen and servants' hall but also a massive laundry room and a still room. The still room was where cakes and what we called fancies were made – delicate pastry creations and suchlike. The people I was working for on the edge of Norwich had to make do with my apple pie and sponge cake.

Like all kitchen maids Daisy got her chance to cook when I had a day or, more rarely, a weekend off. So it was like an apprenticeship really, an apprenticeship that I'd already gone through.

By getting to know the condiments and bowls, saucepans, knives and herbs, and of course by keeping her book, Daisy was quickly getting the hang of it. She was a bit unlucky because in a really big house the scullery maid prepared the vegetables for the kitchen maid to cook for the servants while the kitchen maid prepared the vegetables for the cook to cook for the family – if you follow me! It was split more fairly in a really grand house, but as Daisy had no scullery maid in ours she had to do the whole lot. In the Norwich house Daisy did the washing and cutting and preparation for the family and for the upper servants. It was horribly hard work for her as it had been for me.

The work could have been easier but the upper classes, and even more so the aristocracy, were resistant to new gadgets and labour-saving devices.

Automatic whisks were available before the war, for example. They were not electric but the sort where you turned a handle and a wheel so the whisks went round quickly. We knew about these things but we weren't allowed to use them. Because everything had to be done with a hand whisk, the work took twice or more often three times as long.

But despite all that, by the time war came in 1939 Daisy and I had the kitchen running beautifully. We had more time to sit and have tea together and we even sneaked out together to get the bus to have tea in Norwich when we could. It wasn't often. As I've said, servants 'fraternising' with other servants was frowned on. Maybe they thought we'd hatch a revolution and take over the house! Whatever it was it was based on the idea of divide and rule I'm sure.

In the big house where she'd formerly worked, Daisy had had to put up with all sorts of extra indignities that I never experienced. She told me that whenever the family had been away and were expected back all the servants had to line up in front of the house as the family got out of their cars and walked up the steps to the front door. They also had to attend the chapel attached to the house. 'Twice a bloody week!' was how Daisy put it. And the ultimate indignity according to Daisy was that when one of the daughters was getting married all the maids had to go up and admire the wedding dress during one of the fittings.

'The idea was to give the girl getting married the chance to crow over us poor lumps and to make us see how far above us she was. It was disgusting,' said Daisy.

'She was a princess and we were never going to be – that was the message.' Daisy felt very hard done by sometimes, but then truth to tell we all did.

Daisy had some great stories about that house. She told me she was in the kitchen one Saturday, standing by the huge doors that led into the second kitchen and from there into the garden – when a fox came hurtling through the door and hid under the table.

'The cook was the most ferocious woman I've ever met,' Daisy said, 'but she loved animals and fed several stray cats. When she saw that fox she slammed the door to the garden as the hounds rode up. Then, when the whipper-in knocked on the door she opened up and told him to his face that there was no fox, she hadn't seen it and that there were several cakes in the oven and it was more than her job was worth to let him in the kitchen even to look. And with that she shut the door and let the fox out twenty minutes later. All the maids loved her after that even though she was a dragon!'

Daisy had another great story from that job. Every year there was a cricket match between the village boys and the children of the local gentry and every year – according to Daisy – the locals boys were told they would receive a shilling each if they made sure the gentry won the match!

Chapter Forty-Four

My ignorance of the world would have astonished most people born after the Second World War, but I had no idea about politics in the 1930s. I had no idea about women's rights, and the Great Depression in America was over before I'd hardly heard of it. The truth is I barely knew which party was in government and if Charlie hadn't talked about the coming war I'd have known precious little about that either, unless maybe a bomb had landed in the kitchen.

You see women, but particularly working-class women, were not encouraged to be interested in the world and its affairs then. It was assumed to be a bit above our heads. But Charlie and the war made me realise how the world was changing. What a terrible thing to be in your thirties before you even start to think about things outside your own little world. When I was a girl I hardly knew anyone who managed to live much beyond fifty or sixty, so here I was more than halfway there, and only just finding out things I should have known twenty years earlier.

By the time I was in my seventies, being in your mid forties or even fifties wasn't considered *that* old, but before the National Health Service and pensions came along it was all very different. You were old or dead at fifty.

No one did any exercise when they finished work, everyone smoked cigarettes and drank most days and working people's diets were bloody awful. Working people hated eating vegetables except potatoes, so we were an unhealthy lot except so far as weight goes because I hardly ever saw a really fat person then and certainly not during the war.

It's odd, isn't it, how at a time when people felt so undernourished – I mean during the war – they were probably healthier than they've been since? You see we got so little meat and butter because it was all rationed and you had an ounce or two per person per week, so we had to eat tons of cabbage and potatoes, carrots, sprouts and so on. We had to eat things we could grow here in England easily because all the bananas and oranges vanished for the duration.

It wasn't a great change for servants like us because we had never been able to afford tons of butter and cream for ourselves anyway. It was worse for the family I worked for and for other similar families who were used to having whatever they felt like eating and however much of it they wanted. Her ladyship used to come down during the war and almost beg me to try to make things taste as they had before the war, but it was impossible of course. Everything had been cooked in butter and cream and now it had all vanished. It was margarine, margarine and more margarine!

By 1942, when poor old Norwich was badly damaged by bombing, the food situation had got much worse. I say poor old Norwich because those Nazi devils deliberately bombed it as it had so many lovely old buildings. There were railway goods yards of course and they went for those too, but they were really after the medieval buildings and they destroyed hundreds. It was mindless bloody destruction.

It was mindless destruction in the kitchen too as I increasingly had to make do with scraps and odds and sods. The number of rabbits we ate shot up, as did pigeons, and like a lot of well-connected people, the family I worked for fiddled the system shamelessly.

You see they thought they had been born with an entitlement to a certain standard of living and they really thought that poorer people were better equipped to live on less – even during the war.

I don't think there was any nastiness in it. They just assumed that we had always lived on a few scraps of bacon and lots of spuds and that therefore war shortages weren't so hard for us to bear, whereas for them no butter was a matter of life and death.

So, as the war dragged on, even occasional dinner parties stopped and meals had a dreariness to them, but I was still proud of some of the things I managed to do with dried eggs and spuds, which we all seemed to be eating. We had a fair bit of fish and I used to mash it up with Worcester sauce and potatoes and make fish cakes. It had to go a long way and Daisy called them fish cakes with a difference – the difference being they had no bloody fish in them!

But my nettle soup was a triumph. You needed just the tiniest amount of butter, a great bag of nettle tops and a sniff of cream to make a wonderful soup. In fact it was so good that I carried on making it after the war.

When I first made it in, I think, 1943, her ladyship sent a message down saying how on earth did you find asparagus at this time of year? So again you see when we worked wonders they were sometimes grateful.

Chapter Forty–Five

The war years were terribly dreary, especially in Norfolk, which is all big skies and flat land and when the leaves are gone and the fields are brown you think winter will never end. The war made all of us interested in the outside world. I even read a newspaper now. It was hard to imagine the damage done to London and other cities. Norwich was bad enough.

But about halfway through, in 1943 I think, the house changed. We'd had pretty poor rations like everyone else and then her ladyship told me one morning that she had organised food deliveries from a relative. This sounded very odd to me. Apart from anything else it was extraordinary for an upper-class woman to admit that she had relatives in trade. I didn't believe a word of it, especially as it was always the duty of the cook to order all the food. And there was something about her face that wasn't right when she told me. She looked awkward and I can tell you, no employer ever looked awkward in front of a servant without very good reason. It was a bit of a puzzle – well, it was for a while.

Extra eggs began to be delivered to the kitchen door now and then – and I mean a lot of extra eggs – and large parcels of meat would come pretty regularly. Then the penny dropped. It was all black-market stuff. When the grocer delivered in the normal way you knew there would be a bill at the end of the week or the month, but after the meat and eggs and butter started to arrive they were delivered by a man I'd never seen before and there were never any bills – or at least none that came to me.

He would just drop everything on the big kitchen table and leave without a word. The amounts were pre-war quantities – huge joints, and butter by the pound.

I think her ladyship had made an arrangement, not with a shopkeeper as I'd thought at first, but with a relation who owned a large estate in Suffolk. Soon there were no more complaints about the food and no one came down to see me to beg me to do my best with what little we had. But I was told by her ladyship in a note rather than in person that the servants' meals should continue to reflect 'the current rationing situation'.

In other words the mean old devil wanted me to continue to cook spuds and cabbage for the other servants while the family enjoyed all the black-market stuff. Well, I'm afraid I took very little notice of that I can tell you. If her ladyship was having black-market stuff, we were all having it and so much of it arrived that I don't think she would ever have noticed that I wasn't keeping it all for the family anyway. From now on till the end of the war it was, as far as the food went, as if there wasn't a war on at all. I suppose I should have shopped them but I'd have lost my job and the police were very wary of important local families and wouldn't have done anything anyway.

Charlie used to say, 'It would need to be murder with fifty witnesses in broad daylight in the middle of high summer for the local toffs to end up in court and even then the arresting bobby would take his hat off and ask permission to make the arrest.'

The assumption was always that the well-born found it impossible to do anything criminal.

It was all this black-market stuff that got me into trouble in the end and in a way that, looking back, I still find astonishing.

Towards the end of the war I'd got used to the regular arrivals of parcels of black-market meat and butter and cream so I hardly paid attention when one day early in 1945 a man I'd never seen before came to the kitchen door and offered to 'leave a big ham' as he put it. I just thought it was part of her ladyship's arrangement – particularly as the deliveries were not always made by the same man anyway – and it was no longer anything to do with me.

I told him to leave the ham on the kitchen table so he did. But a week later he came with another ham and asked to be paid for the first. He must have thought I was mad when I told him I didn't think that was the arrangement. He very gently said that he couldn't leave till he'd been paid so in a terrible fluster I told him I would see her ladyship in the morning – which I still did pretty much every morning – and sort out his money.

I couldn't just dash upstairs and have a word. It was unthinkable to do anything like that so I thought I would wait for our regular meeting.

When her ladyship knocked on the kitchen door in the morning I had the little tablecloth on a small table ready and we sat for a while together. I'd never really looked at her much before because servants were not supposed to. You could look but there was an art to looking for a second and then looking down so as to indicate who was superior to whom. Looking for too long would have been seen as insolent. There was a status even in where and how you looked at people. But this morning I was so flustered about having to tell her about the strange man who'd come for his money – thinking it was probably all my fault – that I absent-mindedly gazed at her. I noticed how much she'd aged in the years I'd worked for her and I wondered and thought how strange that we should have known each other all these years and yet we knew nothing at all about each other. Perhaps she was as trapped by it all as I was.

In all my time in the house I had seen the dining room only on one or two occasions. I'd never ever been in the sitting rooms or drawing room let alone in the bedrooms, the study or the library. I had no idea what she did or said upstairs, what she was interested in or who her friends were. But there we are. That was the world we lived in and it seemed nothing could change it. All that could happen was what eventually did happen: it simply died out.

Anyway, after we'd discussed the menu for the day I mentioned the man who'd arrived the day before asking to be paid.

'He left a large ham,' I said, 'and I assumed it was just the usual delivery.'

But even as I said this I knew it must have sounded ridiculous because I didn't know his name and I should have checked he was making the usual delivery organised by her ladyship. I explained all this carefully as we sat there. I said I'd realised that the man making the delivery was not someone I recognised but that he had behaved as if everyone was expecting him. It was all very strange and I knew there was a problem when her ladyship immediately looked almost panic-stricken. She didn't blame me but she said, 'Pay him if he comes again, and then say we want nothing else.'

About an hour later the man turned up and he was all smiles and charm. He said he'd been baffled when I'd said I hadn't expected to pay him. He said he thought I would understand that the ham was off the 'back of the proverbial lorry' and that he was selling it.

'I'd love to give it to you, darling,' he said. 'But how would I live then?'

He said he'd been discharged from the army after being wounded in action and that he'd struggled to make a living after returning to civvy street. Selling black-market meat was a last resort. He hated doing it but had no choice.

I thought I was a shrewd customer but actually, as I've said, I wasn't all that worldly and I completely fell for all this. He just had a way about him and, truth to tell, in his easy ways he reminded me of my father – always a fatal thing in a woman who has happy memories of her dad.

So after about ten minutes we were chatting away and I'd given him a cup of tea and a biscuit. I paid him for the bacon and he said it was too much and he wasn't in the least offended when I told him we couldn't buy anything else.

I felt I'd had a narrow escape from a terrible predicament when he left but there was something charming about him and when he turned up a week later I had to admit I was rather pleased.

When I answered the door he was all smiles and held

his hands up and said, 'Before you say a word I promise I'm not here to try to sell you anything – I won't even give you a present. I was just worried we'd got off on the wrong foot and I wanted to apologise as I felt I'd put you in an awkward position. I know what it can be like as my sister is in service.'

And then the devil pulled his master stroke. He must have known I would still be a bit wary, so he said, 'Right, I must be on my way. Very good to see you again.' And he tipped his hat and was gone.

After a bit I began to feel I'd been too harsh on him and that I should at least have asked him in for a cup of tea, which I often did with the tradesmen who delivered things and indeed with the black-market people. He'd turned up and been very polite and then gone away quickly without pestering me to buy anything and I'd almost scowled at him. I felt so guilty I thought, If he turns up again I will ask him to have a cup of tea to make up for it.

It was something I later bitterly regretted but it's so easy with hindsight to realise how you've been tricked and some con men will trick almost anyone however smart they are. And if nothing else Joe was a great con man.

So Joe started to call in every week or once a fort-night at least. Sometimes he called in twice in a week. He was always very polite and almost timid. He was good-looking, dark and thin, just like the villain in a play, which is what he turned out to be. But of course, starved of male company as I was and still missing Charlie, I started to look forward to Joe's visits. He wasn't like Charlie – I mean he wasn't the life and soul – but he was one of those people who seem to be so interested in what you're saying that it makes you feel really good about yourself and, apart from Charlie, I hadn't really had much attention in my nearly forty years of life.

After a few months he'd got me so hooked I was almost bloody mothering him! I started to give him pieces of cake when he came round and he told me all sorts of stories about his life in the army and how he'd been shelled while fighting in France.

He was so convincing and some of what he told me might well have been true but I think most of it was probably made up for my benefit.

After a few months he suggested I might like to go to the playhouse in Norwich and before I knew where I was or what I was doing I'd said yes. And I must admit I was excited like a green schoolgirl. Daisy was the only one who thought something wasn't quite right. She said, 'I know it's none of my business but there's something funny about that feller Joe who's always calling in to see you.'

'He's all right,' I told her, 'and he only comes for a cup of tea and a chat. No harm in that.' But I didn't tell her I was going to meet him away from the house.

A few days after I'd made my little date with Joe, Daisy said, 'You're very happy, aren't you?'

'What do you mean?' I said

'Well, you've been smiling and humming away to yourself for days now!'

'Have I?' I said, but I think I went red in the face because I hadn't really been aware of it at all.

I tried to make light of it but she was right. I would have given her a scolding – in fact I wanted to because she'd embarrassed me, but we were really good friends by this time so I couldn't.

A bit of me thought that at my age I shouldn't be doing this cloak and dagger stuff but apart from a bit of painting and chatting to Daisy I spent my whole time cooking for other people, which wasn't a huge amount of fun. I still wanted some life before it was too late. But I think another part of me realised that if I couldn't tell Daisy then there must be something wrong, but there's none so silly as a silly old woman in love so I went on with it anyway.

Chapter Forty-Six

We saw a play in Norwich. I have no memory now of what it was but for me it was exciting just to be taken out. The truth is I was vulnerable to any attention because I hadn't had much up to now. I'd have gone out with a kettle if it had asked me and that really is the only excuse I've been able to offer myself for my stupidity.

So after the play we then went for tea and he came on the charabanc – we really did call the bus a charabanc back then – and he saw me home before doing his usual trick of tipping his hat and disappearing.

We had tea together just as usual when he came round about a week after our date and I was so smitten by now that I didn't even worry that her ladyship might catch us in the kitchen – all caution seemed to have gone. Perhaps I had it in mind that I could have lied to her in an emergency and said he was a tradesman or something, but the need never arose.

We had a few more dates and then something odd and unexpected happened.

We were just sitting talking and staring out the tea-shop window when he asked for the bill. Then, when it arrived, instead of paying as he always insisted on doing

201

– despite my attempts to pay at least some of the time – he told me he was a bit hard up at the moment and could I help him out. He said it so sweetly and openly that I immediately paid the bill and told him he must let me pay more often.

We'd been going for our little trips for a while now and I didn't want him thinking he had to pay for everything. In fact we had a bit of a joke about it and I was rather pleased because I thought it meant we'd got closer to each other now that we could laugh about who paid for what. But looking back the really odd thing about all this was that Joe never tried to kiss me or put his arm round me in all those weeks and months. All right, I wasn't Greta Garbo or Jane Russell but even I was beginning to ask myself why he was seeing me if he didn't even want to kiss me. It was a mystery and it's amazing how a woman in middle age can convince herself that all's well when it so obviously bloody isn't. I said to myself, 'Well he's probably just a bit shy.'

How could I have been so silly? If there was anything he was definitely not, it was shy.

But at the time I thought no more about it and just looked forward to him popping around again. I never asked where he went or what he did when he wasn't with me, and again looking back I realise that was a bad sign. He was the sort of person you just couldn't ask those sorts of questions.

Anyway, next time we met he said we should just have a walk round the town. He said his latest business venture had gone wrong and he found himself with no money at all. I told him not to worry and that I was happy to pay whenever we went out, which I was, so we traipsed off to a little café and generally carried on as usual. Then, when we'd had our tea and he was having a smoke and looking completely relaxed, he just casually asked if I could lend him five pounds.

'I hate to ask,' he said, 'but you've been so kind and I could certainly pay you back at the end of the week.'

I was a bit startled by this because people in those days very rarely tried to borrow money from each other because we were all too poor and you guarded carefully what was yours because you knew that without money and savings if you fell on hard times you were in deep trouble.

Whenever I thought I might one day have no money the nightmare of the old woman breaking stones on the road – the woman I'd helped as a child – came into my mind. It was a frightening prospect. So for all the years I'd been working I'd steadily saved my money with the idea that I could one day buy my little cottage. It had always been my dream and it was almost more important to me than meeting a man who might marry me. I wanted somewhere of my own so that maybe even before I retired I might be able to have my own life and not have to work as a live-in cook. Living in was a bit like being in prison because you were at their beck and call day and night and nothing was truly yours – not even your bloody bed.

So I guarded my savings jealously, but I was completely besotted with Joe and when he said he'd pay me back at the end of the week, like a fool I believed him. Five pounds was a lot of money in those days – especially for a servant – but what could I do? I felt I had to say yes. I felt it was a test of my trust and affection for him. I was still like a bloody soft schoolgirl despite my age. So I told him to call next day at the house and when he did, I handed him five of my precious one pound notes.

Well, the end of the week came round and no sign of Joe. Two weeks later he turned up all smiles and about mid-afternoon, just at the time he knew things would be quiet in the kitchen and I'd be able to give him tea.

I was hopeless at getting angry with him. He didn't apologise for not coming back when he had said he would to repay the five pounds. And as usual there was not a word about where he'd been or what he'd been up to. But he was as friendly as ever and hardly seemed to notice that I was a little nervous and worried. In fact he deliberately ignored it, I'm sure. I knew that if I said anything it would look as if I was spoiling our time together.

When he left after the usual half an hour or so he suggested we meet for tea the following week on my afternoon off and I just said yes because I was too silly to say no.

I should say that, like most women then, I'd been brought up to defer to men. My mother deferred to my father. He was a nice man and didn't ever take advantage of her, so I just didn't know how to deal with Joe, who, it seemed, was only going to be nice to me if I never mentioned the money he had borrowed.

Of course I should have mentioned it when we next met but somehow I couldn't. He made me feel mean and petty. The truth is I was afraid of him by now and didn't want to meet him at all but I felt I'd led him on which was something girls – and even women of forty – were always warned against. So I'd landed myself in a right old pickle. I couldn't talk to Daisy about it as I was supposed to be her boss and it was embarrassing if I talked to her as a friend as I was much older and was supposed to know more than she did, not less.

When Joe and I met the next time I was almost frightened, but he was charm itself and we went to our usual tea shop having got the bus into Norwich. He sat there in a sort of smart dark overcoat, shirt and tie, smoking and laughing and talking perfectly naturally while I sat and tried to join in. I remember what happened next as if it was yesterday, though Joe is long dead now.

He said, 'I'll get this tea but I really need another five pounds and I'm sure you won't miss it, especially when you think of all the teas I've paid for. Don't worry, I don't need it now. I will pick it up when I call for tea in a couple of weeks.'

And then he gave me a very direct but odd look – it made me feel threatened. It was a just a pause and a look but it was really frightening.

I was half terrified and half furious because I felt bullied, which I hated, so I just smiled and said, 'I'm sure that will be all right.' We then talked of other things and walked to the bus stop together.

I hardly spoke all the way back but he chatted away as if nothing had happened. I thought of what a dope I'd been.

There was something about Joe that made me too scared to say anything or refuse him anything and the penny had dropped too late: he clearly had no romantic interest in me at all. I felt so sorry for myself partly because I was ashamed. I thought I was a silly middle-aged woman who had jumped at the first man who came along. 'You deserve all you get, you silly cow,' I said to myself.

I couldn't sleep that night and had a terrible week

worrying, but I resolved that whatever happened I wouldn't give him any more of my hard-earned money. Five pounds had already disappeared and it had taken me a long time to earn that money.

I know it sounds like an extreme thing to do but I decided the only thing to do to get away from him was to leave my job and go and work somewhere else where he wouldn't be able to find me. I told her ladyship the very next morning when she came down to discuss the menu that I was going to leave as soon as possible. I didn't dare say what had happened to me. I just said I had to leave at the end of the week for urgent personal reasons and asked if I could be excused any further notice period. She told me she was very sad to lose me and actually she was really very nice and asked if it was a question of money or if she could do anything to help. I told her that I just felt I had to move on and I think she could see that I meant it.

When Joe turned up all smiles for his tea the following week I got Daisy to say I was ill but that I would see him the week after that.

While she talked to him I stayed on the other side of the door into the pantry and I could tell from his tone, even though I couldn't hear exactly what was being said, that he was angry.

When he had gone and Daisy came back in she said:

'I don't think he believed a word I said. He was furious and said to tell you that he will be back next week and the week after that if necessary.'

Daisy didn't know about my troubles – or at least not all of them – but she made me smile when she said, 'I told him you were ill, but I wasn't nice to him and he could see it. I wanted to spit in his eye to tell the truth. I told him that I had important work to do and couldn't stand there all day discussing the price of figs with someone who had nothing to do with the house.'

That was when Daisy was at her loveliest. I couldn't help it but I gave her a kiss and she gave me a hug. She was telling me in her own way that she knew he was making me unhappy.

I just can't explain what a fright I was in by this time but I could see my way out and I was determined to take it. The next day I told Daisy I was leaving and that I'd told her ladyship. Poor Daisy was horrified and thought it must be something she had done. I told her it was to do with Joe. I didn't give her the details, but of course she knew enough after that incident at the door. She shook her head and said, 'I knew he was a bad one,' and of course she'd been right all along.

After that I had to move quickly. I got a reference from her ladyship and took it to a domestic servants' agency in Norwich. I was lucky as it was an excellent reference and I was offered a new job on the spot. Her ladyship wasn't pleased when I reminded her that I had to leave very soon but we agreed I could go in two weeks. I told her she could keep back some of my money as it was such a short notice period but I think she could see I was in a state.

Daisy put Joe off again by telling him that I'd had to go and see a relative who was ill. Before Joe was back a week after that I was gone and I moved to a job as cook at a big house very close to King's Lynn, which was not far from the royal family's house at Sandringham. Best of all, King's Lynn was more than forty miles from Norwich!

The pay was very good in my new job. I was to cook for a retired civil servant who had worked in India for many years. He and his wife wanted me to live in but I'd had enough of that by now. I was going to live out. I was absolutely insistent on that even if it did mean spending my savings bit by bit on a rented room. It would still be better than being under the family thumb day and night, seven days a week, and God knows I'd been in that position long enough by now.

Chapter Forty-Seven

When I left my old job I made sure that I didn't tell Daisy where I was moving to and I didn't tell her ladyship either. I was so terrified that Joe would find me that I didn't dare. Poor Daisy thought I hated her and her ladyship thought I'd gone mad. But I thought that if anyone knew he would be bound to find out. I was sure he would find a way to winkle it out of anyone – he was such a brilliant con man.

Why on earth didn't I just threaten him with the police? you might ask. Well, the reason is that I thought he hadn't really done anything illegal at all. If I'd told anyone what he had done up to then – anyone except Daisy that is – they'd have thought I was completely off my head. It would be said that I'd encouraged him. I'd agreed to lend him the money, after all. He'd never hit me or anything so what was I going to tell them? That there was just something menacing about him? That he had a sort of threatening way about him? I knew no one else would see it because he could turn the intimidating manner on me and the charm on everyone else. He could turn the one off and the other on in a minute. Also I knew that if I didn't get away I would have to give him more money and I wasn't going to do that.

The great thing was that no one knew me in King's Lynn. I somehow knew I'd be safe and he'd never find me. Of course I had my work cut out to get away in time before he found out. I got all my belongings in two big suitcases – two suitcases after all my years working. Pitiful, wasn't it? But at least it made it easier to find somewhere to stay.

So I arrived at my new job mid-morning, intending to leave my suitcases in the kitchen and explain that I needed the rest of the day to find somewhere to live. Now twenty-five years earlier you couldn't have dictated terms like this, but cooks were becoming hard to find and so employers were more accommodating. People found that if they weren't nice to their servants, the servants upped and left and went to work somewhere else or gave it up altogether and went to work in a factory or a shop where they could earn a bit more and not suffer what used to be called the shame of the servile cap. The servant's cap was like the symbol of everything servants hated about their work.

The kitchen maid let me in. She looked at me as if I was stark naked and then ran to tell the mistress of the house that I'd arrived. I'm sure the poor maid thought I was a mad thing turning up like that. But when I saw the mistress I thought, no one will think I'm eccentric compared to someone dressed like that!

She had on a sort of turban with red and yellow streamers coming off it and dangling halfway down her back. This was a time when middle-aged, middle-class women wanted above all to be respectable, so they nearly always dressed in pretty sombre clothes. But here was this woman about six feet tall dressed in a blue and red dress down to the ground – it was a striped dress too

– and it was only later I realised it was more like two dresses with the topmost one sort of cut through to allow the bright blue to show through from underneath. She really did look like a big, exotic bird. When she saw me all drab and plump and mouse-like in the hall she rushed up to me like a tea clipper with all her sails billowing behind and said in a voice like a navvy, 'What can you mean? Surely you wish to stay here while you are with us? I mean live here with us? We have a lovely room for you. Perfect in every way.' She pronounced 'every' as if it had fifteen Rs in it. One minute her voice was so low she sounded like a man and then it would become squeaky and high-pitched. What with her appearance and her voice it was very hard to concentrate when she talked to you.

I was already flustered by my escape and all that had happened to me in the past few months, but I wasn't going to give in. I was a stubborn old thing when push came to shove. And I knew straight away that my new boss wasn't a tough old bird at all. Though she sounded very grand there was something in her manner that was completely unthreatening. I think it was to do with the fact that her eccentricities hid quite a shy, unsure woman. She was also completely unselfconscious and I got the feeling that she thought I was a valuable asset rather than another skivvy to be bossed about and talked down to. I can't explain why I felt this but I did. I'd had enough by now of living in so I stuck to my guns, thanked her for the offer but insisted I would live out. This had been explained by the agency anyway so I'd been surprised when she suddenly tried to make me change my mind. I suspect she was so eccentric that she'd completely forgotten the terms under which I was coming to her. But she quickly saw I was determined and she agreed to let me spend the rest of that day looking for lodgings.

If she hadn't agreed to me living out I would have gone off there and then and looked for something else, because I had enough savings to survive for at least six months without a job and that gave me courage.

I had all my savings – about £500 – in a tin, would you believe. I never felt happy with banks and I doubt if I could have had a bank account anyway. Domestics just never did because you had to pay to have an account and I was damned if I was going to pay for someone else to mess about with my money and only let me have it when it suited them between ten o'clock and three, which was the only time banks opened back then.

Mrs Howard, my peacock-coloured mistress, lived in an ugly Victorian house with just a kitchen maid, a housemaid and a gardener, but no butlers or footmen. She sounded aristocratic but clearly times were hard.

I found lodgings by walking the streets of Kings Lynn – people very often put up signs in their windows saying 'room to let', so finding somewhere wasn't going to be as difficult as it sounds or as it would have been thirty years later. I also looked in shop windows where people put cards. The war was over by now and almost all the houses were drab and looked as if they hadn't been painted in decades. The fact is that no one had any money. To make ends meet almost everyone who could, would try to rent out a room or two in their house. Tramping the streets was the usual way to find lodgings even for people like me who were getting on a bit. And there was no shame back then in renting, as there was later, because house buying was beyond the reach of the poor.

Eventually I found a two-storey house in a quiet street with a sign in the window saying 'Rooms to let – no children' and I just knocked on the door. It was as simple as that.

By late afternoon I was in my little room and being given tea by my new landlady who seemed a nice old thing. Looking back I realise that life was really all about bloody tea in those days. Whenever you had a minute off or a date or you met someone for the first time it was straight to the teapot. No one ever drank coffee that I can recall. It was considered French or – worse – Italian, and therefore immoral!

Anyway, Mrs Shepherd, my new landlady, told me she was delighted to have someone else in the house. She'd been on her own for six months, ever since her last lodger left. She was a widow and I sensed we'd get on really well – largely because she sat right down and had her tea *with* me, rather than plonking a cup in front of me and retreating to her bit of the house.

We sat in her sitting room or parlour as she liked to call it. The walls were covered with old pictures of Queen Victoria and there was an upright piano in the corner with a sort of fringed tablecloth over the top of it. There were two or three other small side tables, each with a tablecloth right down to the ground. On the mantelpiece, the tables, the window sills and anywhere else anything would fit – there were knick-knacks, mostly souvenirs from seaside towns all over the country. When I got to know her I discovered she had never visited a single seaside resort anywhere. The origin of her ornaments was to remain a mystery.

I never knew much about antiques or pictures – apart

from those I had painted – but the stuff she'd accumulated in addition to the seaside ornaments was the biggest load of junk you can imagine. It was all absolutely covered in dust and clearly hadn't been cleaned or moved in years. Mrs Shepherd used to say whenever we met on the stairs or had tea or breakfast together, 'I wouldn't give a cleaner the time of day. You're always better to do it yourself otherwise your precious things will disappear or be broke.'

Well that was the funniest story anyone ever heard because Mrs Shepherd never cleaned any part of the house or anything in it in all the time I knew her. When we had breakfast together I tried to eat the least amount I could because I was convinced everything was filthy. And it was fatal to look at the plates or spoons as they were certain to have yesterday's dried food on them. I was sure I'd be poisoned in the end but in so many ways Mrs Shepherd was such a nice old thing that I couldn't bear to offend her by letting her see me wipe a spoon on my skirt or refuse a piece of mouldy toast!

In the weeks after that first day in my new home I went from a feeling of happiness at having my own place – even if it was in someone else's house – to terror that that black-hearted devil Joe would catch up with me. One day I'd think I was safe, the next I'd be sure he'd turn up on the doorstep. And I had nightmares about him sitting next to me on the bus to work or bumping into me walking along the streets.

It's a funny thing but when you are frightened you lose the power to think straight. Even though I knew there was virtually no way Joe could find out where I'd gone, I still spent weeks looking behind me as I went about the streets and particularly as I went in the door of the house in the evenings. I always walked quickly from the bus stop, too, and would take different routes on different days. And I was so amazed years later that I could have been so fearful about that one thing when I'm not normally fearful at all. The truth is he was a bit of a demon and I had little experience of men. He put me off men for life, despite my earlier luck with Charlie. But I never had any other offers so it didn't matter much anyway.

It was at this time that I learned an important lesson that I should have learned years before: if you leave a servant's job in a hurry there is a good chance you'll end up with a job you don't like.

In a moment of madness before I took the job at King's Lynn I had thought about going to London but Daisy had told me it was awful there. How she knew was beyond me because she'd never been within fifty miles of London in her life, but London's reputation wasn't good. I imagined I'd be stuck in a maze of streets that stretched for tens of miles in every direction with not a bit of green to be had anywhere. I had heard that the only gardens in many places were squares where the householders had a key but it was a strict rule that no servant was ever allowed to borrow the key and sit in the garden. So I didn't like the sound of that at all. And though I might have complained in winter at the brown empty fields of Norfolk stretching away to the horizon, the countryside sort of seeped into you if you were a country girl like me and you knew you'd miss it if it wasn't there.

The other thing about London back then was that country people really did think they would be corrupted in some way if they went there. This was especially true among us Norfolk Methodists. We were convinced London was nothing but prostitutes and robbers and that the prostitutes were robbers as well! And that was why I never got to London. It was too big an adventure for me.

My duties in the new house included paying the female staff. That was a new one for me but it was a job the cook sometimes had to do, and besides there was only a housemaid and a kitchen maid. I also had to order all the food, tell the gardener what to dig up each day and cook three, sometimes four meals a day. The kitchen maid was experienced but I had a feeling we wouldn't get on and we didn't, at least not at first. I was so used to Daisy, who just knew what to do without me saying a word, that I felt it would be difficult to get used to anyone else.

One of the difficulties was that in this house I was supposed to use a cookery book that was kept propped up with its pages open in a kitchen cupboard with glass panels in the doors. The book looked as if it had been in use for about two hundred years but Mrs Howard insisted I use it. She also insisted on opening the glass cupboard doors each day, turning the book to the page she wanted and then locking the doors again. I wasn't allowed to have the key to the cupboard but had to check the recipes on the page through the glass. She hoarded the key to the cupboard as if it were the key to a pot of gold.

Mrs Howard was very aristocratic-sounding as I've said, but I think she might have been foreign or had lived abroad for a long time because she often said, 'I adore English cooking' – words no Englishwoman would ever have uttered. As well as being very tall – at least six feet

I should think – she always wore her high turban or any one of a series of extravagant hats with tall bright feathers, even in the morning. Most of the time she was so colourful she looked like a gypsy. Over the coming weeks I discovered that despite her odd ways she was really very friendly. She would smile at me whenever we discussed the day's menu and popped down into the kitchen whenever she fancied it – sometimes several times a day. She even patted my arm once, which astonished me, as no upper-class Englishwoman would have done that to a servant. Her ladyship, my previous mistress, would rather have died than touch me.

The other thing that was eccentric about this house was that the master used to come down regularly and just stand and stare at the kitchen around him. He was a very nice man but on my first day his wife explained how things were run, including how her husband should be treated.

'My husband was badly hurt in the first war,' she said, 'and he has never really recovered. He doesn't sleep well and he tends to wander round the house and the gardens at odd hours and he may make some odd noises or talk to himself but you mustn't worry. He may want to speak to you or he may not. He may spend some time in the kitchen.'

Well, this was a rum go and it got even rummer when I read more of the cookery book in its little specially built cupboard. I straight away realised that I'd have a hard time cooking their meals. There were lots of things in here I'd never cooked before: bœuf bourguignon for example, and tripe à la mode. I was famous for my steak and kidney pudding so this was going to be a right bloody challenge. But I thought to myself, There's no going back my girl. You've just got to get on with it. So I did. I had to put my kitchen maid straight on a few things first but I hope I was fair about it. I said, 'You may have done it in such-and-such a way before and there is nothing wrong with that, but as I've got to do the cooking itself I won't be able to manage at all if we don't do it my way. But I promise I will help you and you can add my recipes to the ones you already know.'

It was at this point that she admitted she had never heard of keeping her own book. I thought this was a terrible thing – and I told her so. It was the traditional way to get on and avoid being a kitchen maid for the rest of your life. So, as a bit of a gesture, I bought her a book in the town and gave it to her as a present. She was delighted, I think, and she told me later she'd never been given a present before, at least not since she was a child. So after that she was on my side and we got along well, though I still missed Daisy.

For a while things went well in the new job. It was a fair old walk – forty minutes or more – from my lodgings to the house but I loved the sense that I was free now and had my own place.

At Mrs Shepherd's my little paintings soon went up on the walls of my room and though she was a bit of an eccentric I got on very well with my landlady.

Best of all was that I knew that at the end of the day, even if it was at eight or nine o'clock in the evening, I could escape and however much my employers might want a sudden meal or hot chocolate at three in the morning, they knew I wasn't there so they bloomin' well couldn't have it!

* * *

Despite her friendly nature cooking for Mrs Howard and her husband started to get more difficult after a few months. It was always the way – you'd start off thinking it was all right and then the nightmares and lunatics would appear!

I was in the kitchen one morning and had just finished making the breakfast. I was beginning to think about lunch when Mr Howard appeared without a word through the door that led upstairs to the main part of the house.

He had his newspaper in one hand and his pipe in the other. I'd only seen him perhaps twice before and I was struck by how conventional he was compared to his wife. He always wore the same black suit and looked somehow tightly buttoned-up in it and a little uncomfortable.

I immediately stood to attention when he appeared but he just smiled at me and walked over to a chair we kept by the window.

He sat down and asked for a cup of tea. He asked very politely, though of course if he had bellowed out the order like Hitler I'd have still got it for him. When I gave him his tea I thought he would go back upstairs but he sat there and read his paper instead. I stood stock-still, thinking what the hell do I do now? It was rare enough for the mistress of the house to come downstairs other than to agree the day's menu but for the man of the house to come down and make himself at home was unheard of – or at least I'd never heard of it. So it was a kind of stalemate. I stood and stared at him and he sat and read the paper. Then, after a few minutes, he looked up, smiled and said, 'Do carry on with your work. I don't want to disturb you.' But of course he was disturb-ing me. After thirty years and more of cooking in one way and under more or less the same conditions this was impossible. It wasn't that he was doing anything unpleasant and I never thought for a moment that he had been sent to spy on us, but I knew I wouldn't be able to cook properly while he was there. Lottie the kitchen maid said he'd done this before now and then and my predecessor hadn't liked it but had put up with it.

'It's cos they're foreign I think,' said Lottie. 'They have different ideas.'

I tried to get on with my work and I know I was the one being difficult, but having Mr Howard sit there even though he was not watching me was the hardest thing I'd had to endure in all my long years in service. I was making a cake and thought to myself, I'm just going to have to get used to this. Then I thought I would mention it to Mrs Howard in the morning, which is what I did. In the meantime Mr Howard carried on sitting in his chair by the window with Lottie and me tiptoeing round him and giving each other looks now and then. After maybe half an hour Mr Howard got up and left without a word.

Next morning Mrs Howard and I sat at the little table opposite each other and once we'd agreed the menu for the day – she opening and shutting the cupboard as usual – she got up to go and I took my chance.

'Could I have a word with you about something else?' I asked.

She immediately sat down and reached across the table and put her hand on mine which nearly put every possible thought out of my head.

'Please tell me you don't want to leave already,' she said.

'No no,' I said, and by now I was in a bit of a panic.

'It is just that I have been a cook so long and have never had to work while being watched by a member of the family.'

'What do you mean?' she said. 'I do not disturb you, do I?'

'It's not you, it's your husband,' I said. 'He came down for about half an hour yesterday and sat reading his paper while I was trying to get lunch ready.'

'And you don't like it?' she said, as if I'd turned down a holiday for two in California.

'It's not that I don't like it, it's just that it is very difficult to work with him there. It's a worry because he may want something or dislike the noise of whisking and pots and pans and me giving orders to Lottie and that sort of thing.'

Then she did a very odd thing. She leant back in her chair, swept her hat off and leant forward again holding her hat in her hand. I was so surprised I nearly jumped up and ran out of the house. Underneath that mad yellow hat was a head of damp-looking and very flattened grey hair.

She said in a whisper, 'I think I mentioned that my husband had some terrible experiences in the first war and so I try to let him do as he pleases as it is good for his mind. I think he likes you. He has said so. But I don't think he will disturb you often. What if I were to pay you an extra £2 a month just to ignore him?'

She smiled and she reached across the table and rested her hand on mine again.

I was all of a dither now because I saw my cottage-buying tin filling up more rapidly if I said yes to this proposal. An extra ten shillings a week was a lot of money back then so I thought, Why not? For that sort of money, and he's nice enough, I will make him twenty cups of tea a day and juggle the dinner plates at the same time.

So that was that. I went back to work and Mrs Howard swept out through the door and back upstairs. To begin with her husband turned up maybe once or twice a week but gradually the visits increased until he was coming every day – and do you know I actually didn't mind a bit in the end.

On one occasion I found him already sitting in the kitchen when I started work at half past six in the morning. He was definitely a bit dotty but he would sometimes talk about the war and his life and we just had to listen. But he'd had such a terrible time of it you'd need to be made of stone not to be sympathetic.

He said he had gradually seen all his friends killed and he'd lain out all night in no-man's-land after being injured with his best friend who was also hurt. I can still remember exactly how he told the tale because he returned to it again and again. Every time he told the tale I remembered poor Charlie in the Second World War.

'We'd started to advance at dawn and our orders were so silly. We'd been told to march in a straight line, not to run or duck or dodge from side to side. There was no need we were told because the bombardment had knocked out the enemy and no one would be there to shoot at us. But within one hundred yards we were toppling like skittles. A man would be hit and just fall forward without a word. The screams seemed to start at night. I remember toppling over as easy as you please. I just couldn't stand up any more and then next to me I saw Tim, my best friend, with the bottom of his jaw missing so he couldn't speak, but he looked at me all the time. My stomach hurt rather badly so I just whispered to him while he looked at me. When I was picked up by the stretcher-bearers Tim was dead, or at least the stretcher-bearers thought he was dead.'

Afterwards he would finish his tea and go back upstairs. On other days he would just talk about the garden or something that had happened in the town.

When I'd started work as a kitchen maid all those years ago the kitchen had been a place the family avoided like the leper hospital. It was beneath their dignity to have anything to do with the preparation of food, the cleaning up and all the mundane back-breaking jobs that had to be done so they could eat. By the 1950s something had got into them, a different spirit that was perhaps partly the result of people's experiences in the Second World War. Mr and Mrs Howard were almost certainly foreign or had lived abroad so that may have been partly why they were just much more relaxed about coming down to see me and talk to me. They even talked to Lottie sometimes which really was an eye-opener.

That's what all the hand touching and smiling was about. I felt a bit of an old curmudgeon for not meeting them halfway as it were and for being suspicious, but perhaps it's not so surprising. After all the rules and restrictions I'd put up with in the early days I didn't really trust anyone who employed me not to turn suddenly back to the old ways of doing things.

But it seemed that Mr Howard really needed his outings to the basement kitchen. He never said whether he enjoyed coming down but there was something about the atmosphere that perhaps calmed his nerves.

One day he asked me to show him how to make a cup of tea as he had never done it in his life. People were amazed by this when I told them years later but at the time I'd have been more amazed if any man I worked for knew how to make a cup of tea.

Mr Howard was charm itself about it.

'Mrs Jackman,' he said, 'I don't want the shame of dying without ever making tea. How on earth do you do it?'

After I showed him he had a go himself.

'You know, I rather enjoyed that,' he said. 'But please don't mention it to Mrs Howard. She might not be sympathetic.'

I drew the line at showing him how to make a cake and he accepted the defeat despite the fact that he could have ordered me to show him.

'You'll be putting me out of a job soon, Mr Howard,' I said and he laughed.

'Now I wouldn't want to do that,' he said. 'But I'm far too stupid to learn all the other things you do so well.' And with that he was off for his afternoon nap upstairs.

Thank God he doesn't want to sleep down here! I thought.

So a year and more went by and though the job was a bit mad with all these goings-on, I got used to it. Despite my late walks and bus rides back to my lodgings I began to think that the world had changed for the better, I really did. I had a sense that people were a little more tolerant and less inclined to look down on each other than they had been back in the 1930s. We were also perhaps a little kinder.

Here I was almost being treated like a friend of the family by both Mr and Mrs Howard. After he started to turn up all the time for a chat and tea she started to do the same thing, always in her great red-and-yellow hats and her kaftan dresses – if that's what they were. Of course I never really felt they thought of me as an equal. Of course they didn't. They'd no more invite me to dinner upstairs or to meet their friends than they'd invite the bloody cat, but at least they didn't act as if I was a piece of furniture or a machine. Truth to tell, I think they were both a bit lonely as they very rarely had friends round and I was an easy person to be with, even if I say so myself! I also say that because my landlady, Mrs Shepherd, said it so often.

'Nancy, you're too easy for your own good,' she used to say when we went shopping together as we sometimes did. I thought, Yes, I'm an easy person because I've spent most of my life bowing and scraping and never saying what I really think and now the habit has bloody well stuck!

Mrs Shepherd was a pale, strong-looking woman. When I knew her she would have been in her seventies I should think. She never told me her real age. She almost always wore curlers, even when she was going shopping, but she'd wear a hat over them or a scarf when she was in the house. She'd always lived in the same little house where I was now the lodger. In fact, she had been born there and the only work she seemed ever to have done was washing down the front doorsteps of all the houses round about. She never did the insides and always said when I asked her why not:

'I've always done cleaning, but the insides don't agree with me, Mrs Jackman, and they never will. I didn't do them then and I'm not doing them now.'

She seemed to be reasonably well off so I couldn't understand why she got up at six every morning to go step washing. She told me she just couldn't give it up. 'It makes me more myself. I'm like one of those pit ponies as dies when you put it out to grass,' she would say. 'So I'm keeping away from that grassy field as long as I can.'

Mrs Shepherd and I got on very well most of the time and it was lovely for me to have someone to talk to who wasn't in service. She only ever got a bit crotchety if I criticised the rich and well off I'd worked for over the years.

'They know their place and we should know ours,' she used to say. 'It's God's will and we would all get on much better if we didn't start to get uppity.'

That was her favourite phrase I think – 'We mustn't be uppity.' If she went in a shop and someone was rude she'd say, 'They're uppity in there.' Or if one of her friends said something she didn't like she'd say, 'She's grown mighty uppity of late.'

But so long as I didn't criticise what she saw as the natural order she loved my stories about the places I'd worked. I used to tell her about a woman who took money off my wages when I was a kitchen maid for eating too much and she'd just say:

'There's bad everywhere, just don't be bad yourself.'

She had some very strange habits too. If there was a knock on the door she would crouch down and tiptoe into the back parlour having whispered to me, 'Tell them I'm not here. I've gone to see relatives in Leamington.' When I later asked her about her relatives in Leamington she looked at me as if I was mad.

'What questions you ask!' she said. 'Why on earth would I have relatives in Leamington? I've never been there in my life.'

I realised that she had a terror of answering the door.

She'd do it if there was no choice but she always preferred to get me to go if she possibly could. She would always tell me what to say to anyone who knocked and it was always that she had gone to visit relatives somewhere. Sometimes it was Birmingham, sometimes Glasgow, but she rarely returned to the same place twice and as far as I could see she had never actually travelled anywhere at all, though she loved to go to the shops in the town.

So there we were. Two dumpy old women whose sole pleasure was gossiping and going shopping together, but we thought we were lucky. It wasn't like the 1960s and 1970s when women suddenly realised they could be free of all the old constraints. It was a drab time and if you had enough money and clothing and heating you thought you really were lucky because all around there was real poverty. There were a few restaurants and dance halls but most of us just stayed indoors when we weren't working and in the early 1950s most of us didn't even have televisions. We still listened to the wireless.

Chapter Forty-Eight

I didn't know anyone who had a TV or who went on holiday so it didn't feel as bad as it might sound. Young people today always think everyone else is having more fun than they are, but we didn't feel that then. Perhaps I was a bit of a fool and I should have been more determined to get out more and do more. Everyone poor lived what looked like humdrum lives – at least humdrum from the outside. But we'd survived the war. That was the big thing that made people feel content.

I always used to think that, just as in my childhood I'd been surrounded by eccentrics and people who were probably almost mad, it was the same when I grew old. It's always been like that if you have eyes to see. People develop funny little fads and ways of behaving as they get older – like insisting to every caller that you are out or wearing turbans covered with feathers. These fads help get them through the days. We never looked at ourselves and thought, That's a bloody funny way to carry on! I've always thought that almost everyone is more or less mad so it didn't signify much.

The saddest thing about this time for me was that my father died. My mother had been dead for some time and now it was my father's turn. I hadn't seen much of him in recent years. He died in the cottage where I'd been born. I remember the funeral. Half a dozen people from the village came and I recognised one or two who had been boys and girls with me. And I thought about the bones in the charnel house and my mother long buried.

It seemed a very sad end to a human being but it was what we must all come to.

Of course cars were everywhere by now and the roads all tarmacked. The village was an unfamiliar place and I didn't like going back. It was all gone. Soon after my father died our tiny cottage was demolished too and something bigger and more modern put in its place. We were not nostalgic then. Anyone who grew up in a poor village as I did loved it when all the modern things came in, especially houses with gas or electric fires, electric light and best of all – no damp. All old houses were damp because they had no foundations at all. The wet came right up out of the ground, which is why so many old people were rheumatic or arthritic.

And the carts had long gone by now of course. We didn't miss them either although I never really trusted those bloomin' cars. I certainly never thought about getting a car or learning to drive – that seemed like man's work to me, like ploughing or carting.

I know Mr Howard never learned to drive and many of the better-off who kept a car never learned to drive themselves because it was too mechanical for them. As a result driving became something that servants really ought to do, so the wealthy employed chauffeurs. I used to think they might have loved to be behind the wheel themselves and speeding along the roads that weren't at all crowded then. But they still thought it was much the best thing to pay other people to do what they saw as practical things. The chauffeurs of the time were often mechanics too, as their owners were terrified the car would break down. And lying in the dirt under a car trying to fix it was definitely something no gentleman would contemplate.

Chapter Forty-Nine

I felt I had come a long way from that tiny cottage where I was born. When I made my way to work each day I used to joke to myself that I was like any business-woman or commuter. Of course I was sad I had no family left, but what could I do? Mum and Dad were dead, Charlie had been killed and the only other man who'd shown much interest in me turned out to be a bloomin' monster.

But I felt safe now. To have a house or at least a room that you could call your own, that wasn't shared or miserable or up six flights of spooky stairs, was quite an achievement for someone with no education who'd spent her life in service. So I didn't worry about the rest of it – I mean going out and having a good time.

My biscuit tin of savings was mounting up too. Having your life savings in a tin sounds odd now every-one has a bank account, but as I say, banks just weren't for people like me. Then one day I saw an advertisement for Post Office savings which said everything was backed by the government so you couldn't lose your money. Also, unlike the banks, the Post Office wouldn't charge me to look after my money. Best of all, they weren't going to look down on me as they would in a bank.

When I counted my money I knew it would be just a couple of years till I could afford to buy somewhere of my own and I felt so proud when I paid it all into my new Post Office savings account. It was a relief too because I'd become convinced that someone might easily steal it and then where would I be? I might only be able to buy a tiny cottage but I was determined to do it. The very excitement of the idea! Well, I can't express it but it was the most wonderful feeling of my life. I wasn't quite there yet but it was still like winning the pools twice in a row just to have my Post Office book and see the money written down there in official ink.

Then, out of the blue, an amazing thing happened. It was as unlikely as the handkerchief dropped during the play that gives the game away.

Chapter Fifty

It started one summer towards the end of the 1950s when I was at home with Mrs Shepherd. For the first time in my life – and remember I was fifty now – I had asked for a week off work. Mrs Howard had been very kind and immediately agreed. I think she had decided by this time that she needed to keep me happy or I might leave. It was just an impression I got, but whatever the truth of the matter I was brave enough to ask for the time off – unpaid of course – and she was nice enough to let me have it. I wanted a week off for no particular reason other than that I'd never really had any real free time before except late evenings and Sundays and an occasional weekend. By this time Lottie had left and I was a single-handed cook, as we used to say. Lottie hadn't been replaced because the Howards couldn't afford it. They never said as much but it was obvious. Mrs Howard told me she would find someone to cook for her during my week off, but I later discovered that she hadn't been successful so she'd tried to manage on her own and had ended up telephoning her friends to ask how to turn the cooker on!

Anyway, I woke up rather later than usual – about eight o'clock – on the second day of my week off and went downstairs. By this time Mrs Shepherd was always down and bustling about. 'I've never been much of a sleeper,' she used to say. And that was no less than the truth because I often heard her moving about at all hours of the night. Lord knows what she got up to.

But the house was completely silent, with no sign that Mrs S had gone out. It was long past the time she would normally be up and about and by eight-thirty I was worried, so I tiptoed to her room and tapped gently on the door.

When there was no answer I gently pushed the door open and saw her lying in bed in the half-dark of the narrow light coming through the gap in the curtains. For a terrible moment I thought she had died but then I noticed a slight movement. I went over and she was at a strange angle, as if she had started to slide out of bed and couldn't right herself. In fact she couldn't right herself because, as I later discovered, she had had a stroke and been paralysed down one side. I knew something was very wrong so I didn't say a word but ran down the stairs and into the street. Five minutes away I knew there was a doctor's surgery and as this was a weekday I was sure I could get help. The nurse saw me and telephoned for an ambulance and within the hour poor Mrs Shepherd was carried off to the hospital.

From then on I went to see her on my afternoons off and at the weekends when I could. In those days, with the Health Service so new, they kept you in hospital for ages for the slightest thing. Women in childbirth were kept in for two or three weeks and no one was expected to care for their sick relatives at home. But I felt bad about Mrs Shepherd because she had no one else to visit her and when I went she would just stare at me and sort of mumble now and then. Her paralysis was awful and she couldn't speak but I had a feeling her mind was all right – she just couldn't get the words out to say what she felt or needed. It was as if she was pleading for someone or something but I never found out what. I used to just talk to her and hold her hand and she seemed soothed by it. But there were strict hospital visiting times then and a fearsome matron who used to boot everyone out on the dot.

I must admit I was also very worried that I was going to lose my home. This was selfish I know, with Mrs Shepherd lying there in a terrible state, but I'd been happy in Mrs Shepherd's house and felt in my early fifties too old to move again. I know I didn't own it but I loved it and felt more comfortable there than anywhere since I'd left home all those years ago.

Several weeks went by like this and I carried on visiting Mrs Shepherd, who showed no signs of improvement at all. Then I arrived at the hospital one evening and was met at the door of the ward by a nurse who asked me to pop in to see matron for a moment. Matron appeared out of nowhere and we went into her little room. She told me that Mrs Shepherd had died that morning and that, as I was a relative, I would need to sign various papers. I told her that we weren't related and that I had no idea if she had any relatives. And you know that's where the mystery started. I went to see a local solicitor in King's Lynn the following Saturday and explained the position. He told me I should go through Mrs Shepherd's papers and see if I could discover anything. I'm not sure this was legal but I think he thought I was pestering him about an old woman who had nothing anyway and he was just trying to get rid of me. Searching through her papers might have been illegal, but what could I do? The hospital registered the death and I heard no more about it from them. I went through Mrs Shepherd's papers and found absolutely no reference to any family at all. But I found an envelope with Mrs Shepherd's will in it. And in that will she simply said that she wanted her house and its contents to go to Nancy Jackman, her friend.

Now isn't that extraordinary? I sat there hardly thinking I was able to read any more. I thought I must have imagined it but I looked at the will again, folded it up, opened it again and read it again, folded it and then read it again. The will was hardly more than a letter really but there it was all inked in: I leave my house and its contents to my friend Nancy Jackman. I didn't feel elated at first. I felt so sad that she had no one else closer than me. How could she have lived so long and been so little known to anyone? At the funeral there were only half a dozen people, all of them neighbours. I had no idea what to do. I went back to the solicitor and showed him Mrs Shepherd's will which he said was in order and he suggested I put an advertisement in the local paper asking if she had any relatives, but he seemed completely uninterested. I'm afraid I never did put that advertisement in the paper because I was worried that lots of people might just turn up making all sorts of claims. If she'd seen none of her family for so long then they can't have thought much of her. So, expecting almost every day to be turfed out, I went on living in the house and I've never moved since. No one ever turned up to argue about it, so there we are. I always felt I'd robbed Mrs Shepherd's family – if they existed – because my good fortune had arisen as a result of her loneliness.

But life is a rum go and with my lack of family

perhaps we were more alike than I liked to think. If I'd known she liked me enough to leave the house I'd have taken her out more but she gave nothing away in life and seemed content always. I never heard her complain. She seemed interested only in her little house, shopping and pottering about. She made few demands on the world. She was friendly, of course, and as I've said we were friends. But being friends back then always had a sort of stiffness about it. You never got close to anyone. We didn't hug and kiss and tell each other our secrets as youngsters do today. It was the way things were and you can't escape the time you're born into, can you? I know that if Mrs Shepherd were alive today she'd say the same. I often wondered afterwards if she saw something of herself in me. Like her I had no family and having been so long in service I hardly had any friends.

So my life changed completely and my only regret is that I was no longer young, but you can't have everything you want. I bought an annuity, a little pension, with the money I'd been saving for my cottage, and suddenly realised I no longer had to work at all. It was a shock but a lovely feeling too. What a change after all my years of slaving for others! I knew I even had enough to employ a skivvy myself, but I was determined never to do it. I felt at this time that the sooner we all got hoovers and dishwashers and washing machines and did our work ourselves the better. No one should have to waste their life skivvying for people who could quite easily clean up their own mess and cook their own food.

But here's the shocker. After all my complaints about being in service I'm embarrassed to say that by the time I was able to pack up work for good I didn't want to. I still painted a bit and still enjoyed it but not as much as I had when I was young, and I worried I would have nothing to do all day and no one to talk to if I gave up work. I was like that bloody pit pony Mrs Shepherd talked about, put out to grass but pining for the heavy rumble of the carts in the mines.

So I stayed on with Mrs Howard.

I'd grown very stout by now, eating biscuits and butter and all the other lovely things I'd never been able to have as a child and a young woman, and then during the war.

I don't think anyone worried about being overweight right up until the 1960s really. They worried far more if you were thin, because it was just assumed that you weren't getting enough to eat. The poor were thin and the better-off were stout and proud of it.

But I stayed at work – can you believe it! – and Mrs Howard and I almost became friends. We really did. As I've explained she was always a bit unconventional anyway and easier to be with than an English toff might have been. She still would never have asked me upstairs for a cup of tea in the afternoon, but she often came down to talk to me. Like many married couples, she'd long ago stopped talking to her husband, but all the other servants had gone by now and I was more of a housekeeper than just a cook and we both knew I could have the job – or not – on my own terms. I couldn't work out for a long time why I felt better about life until one day I realised it was because I was in control. I chose to keep working but I no longer had to. What a lovely feeling that was and it never left me. It was the great comfort of my old age.

I managed the house – Mrs Howard's house – to suit

me now and had plenty of time to sit in her kitchen and enjoy a cup of tea and a read of the paper. I had almost every weekend off too and worked much shorter hours than I ever had before.

Then almost a year to the day after poor Mrs Shepherd died, something else extraordinary happened. Daisy turned up.

Chapter Fifty-One

It was a Saturday. I was washing up before setting off to catch the bus to work when there was a knock at the door. I had become as isolated as Mrs Shepherd by now but didn't mind a bit living on my own and only having my own company. I'd long ago stopped worrying about Joe turning up and people who came to the door were usually offering to wash the windows or tidy the garden. Occasionally the postman would bring something but that rarely happened to me. If you don't write letters (and I didn't), you can hardly expect to receive any.

I talked to the neighbours of course, and they were usually very nice, but we never went round to each other's houses for lunch or dinner. That was something only the middle classes did.

So I was daydreaming and the knock on the door made me jump. When I opened it, there she was, after all those years. I recognised her instantly even though it was a long time since we'd worked together. She looked older and, like me, a bit fatter, but I'd have recognised that cheeky face anywhere. I couldn't help it: I let out a scream the way a child would, seeing its parents after a month without them. There was no awkwardness between us at all, which later on surprised me, but I think we had always had a sort of understanding that had nothing to do with the work we did or the things we said or even the jokes we shared. We just liked each other in some deeper way I think.

Before I knew what I was doing I'd almost dragged her into the parlour and had the kettle on and my best cake shoved under the poor woman's nose.

We started talking and we didn't stop for an hour, which made me late for work.

I never thought to ask why she was there or how she'd found me. It just seemed like it was meant to happen.

'Would you mind if I stayed for a few days?' said Daisy. 'I'm looking for a new place and I'll get one soon I'm sure.'

'You won't,' I said.

She looked upset for a minute, thinking I meant she wouldn't get a place. But that wasn't what I meant at all.

'Of course you'll get a place,' I said, 'but you're not leaving this house. I have a spare room. Why don't you stay here?'

She smiled fit to burst and we just looked at each other and laughed.

I told her how I'd been left the house and was think-ing of giving up work myself, but I was jabbering like a schoolgirl and I'm sure she didn't take in half the things I said. But she was amazed about the house.

'You have this house? You mean it's yours?' she said, gazing around with her mouth open.

I said I'd tell her all about it that evening but she must make herself comfortable till I got back. I could tell she was tired, but isn't it strange how I trusted her so completely having not seen or heard a word of her in years?

I could hardly concentrate at work that day but the hours passed and I was soon back home again. Daisy had tidied and washed up and even cleaned the bloomin' windows.

'Couldn't look out through all that grime, Dolly,' she said.

It turned out that she had worked in two different houses since I'd last seen her, including the Queen's house at Sandringham. She had some wonderful stories about Sandringham and how the royal family seemed to be obsessed by their gamekeepers.

'Well, they were bound to be even more snooty than your average aristocrat and the pay was even worse,' she said. 'But the keepers could do no wrong. I got so mad at the rubbish pay that I stole a couple of spoons and then panicked that I'd be found out if I tried to sell them so I threw them into a hedge!'

Daisy also told me that a few years before she started work at Sandringham the house had been run according to its own time.

'One of the housemaids told me that when the old king was alive he insisted that all the clocks should be set half an hour fast so he wouldn't be late for his shooting or some such nonsense,' she explained. 'Everyone just had to accept it and try not to get confused!'

She told me that the staff were expected to do absolutely anything they were asked to do. 'We were always running upstairs with tea and cocoa and biscuits at all hours,' she said. 'All the servants except me were mad keen royalists. They'd have got down on the floor to be walked on if a carpet went missing!'

This was the start of the happiest time of my life. Daisy went off to an employment agency and eventually found a job working a few afternoons each week for an elderly invalid who wanted to be wheeled around the town. That meant she was always at home when I got back, which was lovely for me. We had such fun together, particularly after I finally gave up work completely in 1961 after nearly forty years in service. Mrs Howard's husband died and she decided to move to the south coast and that was the end of that. I never saw her again. But then she was hardly going to invite me to go down and stay for the weekend, was she?

I lived with Daisy until her death six years later from breast cancer. Twenty years later I think perhaps something could have been done for her but it was a bad case and the cancer ate her up quickly. I nursed her through it and we became closer then than we had ever been. I held her hand most of the last day when it was clear to me that she was going.

Chapter Fifty-Two

On my last day in service with Mrs Howard an odd thing happened. A gypsy couple came to the door. I wouldn't normally give them anything because I had strict instructions not to, but I always liked the gypsies and it was my last day in service – my last day ever – so I thought I would break all the rules and give them something for luck.

I gave them money, some cakes and a bag of sugar. I always remembered what my mother had said: it was good luck to give the gypsies sugar. But it was the 1950s now and gypsies were abandoning many of their old ways so these gypsies – a young couple – probably thought I was mad. But they were very friendly and delighted by the money if not the sugar.

Then, as I looked down the drive, it was as if I'd gone back fifty years and more. Waiting at the end of the drive I saw they had three children with them and one of them, a little boy, had a song thrush on his shoulder.